CHANTING FROM THE HEART

Chanting from the heart

VOLUME 2

CEREMONIES AND PRACTICES IN THE
PLUM VILLAGE TRADITION

Thich Nhat Hanh
and the
MONKS AND NUNS
of PLUM VILLAGE

PARALLAX
PRESS

BERKELEY, CALIFORNIA

Parallax Press
2236B Sixth Street
Berkeley, California 94710
parallax.org

Parallax Press is the publishing division of
Plum Village Community of Engaged Buddhism

Calligraphy by Thich Nhat Hanh Hanh and Brother Phap Huu
Cover design by Gopa & Ted2, Inc. based on
an original design by Charles Woods and Ayelet Maida
Text design by Gopa & Ted2, Inc.

ISBN: 978-1-952692-39-0
E-book ISBN: 978-1-952692-40-6

Library of Congress Cataloging-in-Publication Data
is available upon request.

1 2 3 4 5 / 27 26 25 24 23

Contents

Introduction

T HE SECOND VOLUME of *Chanting from the Heart* contains the ceremonies and other formal practices.

In the West, Buddhism is not usually understood to be a devotional religion. The Buddha taught devotion as a skillful means to lead us gently into the path of mindfulness, concentration, and insight. In our own time we can understand Buddhism as a way of life or an art of living. Some people see it as a philosophy that can help us understand the meaning of life. The Buddha never wanted to teach philosophy or offer theories or doctrines to explain life and death. He used to say he taught only two things: suffering and the end of suffering (happiness).

If Buddhism is not a devotional path, what is the point of ceremonies and chanting? The basic practice of Buddhism is the Three Trainings: mindfulness, concentration, and insight. Chanting and ceremonies are much more than devotion, though devotion can be there too. Let us take for example the practice of offering incense or lighting a candle. When we light a candle or a stick of incense and place it in the censor we are attentive to every gesture and movement. We hold the incense and place it with both hands to ensure that we are doing this with our whole being. We are aware that we are offering the incense of our heart, which is mindfulness, concentration, insight, the knowledge of liberation, and liberation itself. In chanting, every phrase that we recite can be a teaching helping us water the seeds of understanding and love in our consciousness.

It is in our human nature to want to celebrate important events in the cycle of human life or of the year. This has led us to develop ceremonies.

True Virtue
Plum Village, France
2023

Basic Practices Connected to Ceremonies

Walking Meditation

In the Plum Village tradition many ceremonies are preceded by a session of walking meditation and then sitting meditation. The walking meditation can take place outside and can last for thirty minutes or longer. If those attending the ceremony are new to the practice they will need instruction in the practice of mindful walking. In the Plum Village tradition walking meditation is a very natural way of walking. We walk together in silence led by a sangha member. We keep a distance of not more than a meter between us and go at the speed of the one who is leading. We feel like one body and produce a collective energy of mindfulness. As individuals each one of us is very aware of the contact between the soles of our feet and the earth. We keep our mind and body united by awareness of our breathing. We coordinate our steps with our breathing, taking two, three, or four steps with every in-breath and out-breath. We arrive in every step without being pulled back into the past or forward into the future. With the in-breath you can say to yourself: "arrived," and with the out-breath: "at home."[*]

Sitting Meditation

Before a ceremony there are usually ten to fifteen minutes of sitting meditation. People come silently into the hall where the ceremony will take place and walk mindfully to their cushion or chair. You can join your palms and bow your head slightly just to ensure you are truly present before sitting down and adjusting your posture so that you are comfortable and stable. If you sit on a cushion both your knees should be on the floor. Whether you sit on a cushion or a chair your spine should be straight, your shoulders relaxed. A half smile will relax the muscles on your face. You enjoy the feeling of your breathing, recognizing your in-breath and out-breath by saying silently to yourself: "in, out." You can recognize how your breath is becoming deeper and slower, more calm and more relaxed, and at the same

---

[*]For more on walking meditation, see Thich Nhat Hanh, *The Long Road Turns to Joy*, Parallax Press, 2011.

time your body and mind are more calm and relaxed. Smile to yourself from time to time and dwell in the present moment.

INVITING AND LISTENING TO THE BELL

When the ten or so minutes of sitting meditation are over, the bell master* invites† the bell. There is a training to learn how to invite the bell. Before inviting the bell one must feel present and calm enough to do so. The state of mind of the one inviting the bell will be conveyed to those who hear it. In order to become present, the bell master recites a short verse:

> Body, speech, and mind in perfect oneness,
> I send my heart along with the sound of the bell.
> May the hearers awaken from forgetfulness
> and transcend all anxiety and sorrow.

When it is time to invite the bell and we are calm, we invite what is called the wake-up sound. This is to prepare everyone for the real sound. We take the inviter (the baton) and place it against the rim of the bell without removing it immediately so that a half sound is produced. After one in-breath and out-breath we invite the full sound of the bell. We breathe in and out slowly three times between each sound of the bell.

The sound of the bell is the voice of the Buddha calling us back to our true home. When the bell is invited everyone present stops moving, talking and thinking. We all enter a stream of the energy of mindfulness together and the collective energy is very strong. We stay with the sound of the bell for at least three in-breaths and out-breaths.

JOINING PALMS AND TOUCHING THE EARTH

The practice of folding our palms together in the form of a lotus bud supports our mindfulness and concentration. Traditionally in Christianity the folded hands have been used in prayer. In Asia people greet each other in this way. This is because when we join our palms we feel connected to ourselves. We feel the right side of our body is connected to the left side

---

*"Master" here means the one who has mastered the art of inviting the bell and has been appointed to sit at the bell for the ceremony.
†"Invites" is the word used to mean "help the bell to make a sound."

and our mind is connected to our body. Once we are connected to our self we can connect with those around us.

"Touching the Earth" is the name Thầy has given to the practice of prostration which is a very ancient practice in many traditions both East and West. We begin by joining our palms, placing the joined thumbs against the middle of our forehead and saying to our self: "With my brain." Then we bring our joined palms down to the level of our heart, saying to ourself, "with my heart." Then saying to ourself, "with my whole body," we separate our hands and bow down so that our legs from our feet to our knees, our arms from our hands to our elbows, and our forehead are touching the floor. It is like the practice of yoga; the position of our body calms and clarifies our mind. Our heart is on the same level as our brain and we let go of our usual ways of thinking that separate me from you. The one who bows and the one who is bowed to are no longer separate entities. If we are bowing to the bodhisattva of great compassion, we recognize great compassion in ourself.

If in your community your prefer to omit the practices of joining palms and touching the earth, you may always do so. Thích Nhất Hạnh has said: "To bow or not to bow is not the question." To bow as an outer form without inner content is not the aim of the practice. On the other hand touching the earth can be a deep and meaningful practice that brings insight and transformation.

Basic daily practices

Sitting Meditation

M ANY PEOPLE like to make a daily routine of sitting meditation: in the early morning after rising and/or at night before going to bed.

In Plum Village we begin the session of sitting meditation with a chant. The person who is chanting uses the bell in a specific way which needs to be learned in a monastery or practice center. The chant calls us to come together in our energy of sitting meditation. At the end of the chant the whole community joins in the response: "Namo Shakyamunaye Buddhaya." After the chant the community can practice sitting in silence or a guided meditation.*

MORNING CHANT ♪

The Dharma body is shining brightly as the day dawns. [BELL]
In stillness we sit,
our hearts are at peace,
a smile is on our lips. [BELL]
This is a new day, we vow to go through it in mindfulness
so the sun of insight can rise
and shine in every direction. [BELL]
Noble Sangha diligently bring our minds into meditation.
Namo Shakyamunaye Buddhaya
Namo Shakyamunaye Buddhaya (response) [BELL]
Namo Shakyamunaye Buddhaya
Namo Shakyamunaye Buddhaya (response) [BELL, BELL]
Namo Shakyamunaye Buddhaya
Namo Shakyamunaye Buddhaya (response) [BELL]

EVENING CHANT, *Version One* ♪

Stably seated under the Bodhi tree, [BELL]
body, speech, and mind are one in stillness,

*For guided meditations see Thich Nhat Hanh, *Blooming of a Lotus,* Beacon Press, 2022.

free from views of right and wrong. [BELL]
When we are focused in perfect mindfulness, our true nature
is illumined.
The shore of confusion is left behind. [BELL]
Noble Sangha, diligently bring your mind into meditation.
Namo Shakyamunaye Buddhaya
Namo Shakyamunaye Buddhaya (response) [BELL]
Namo Shakyamunaye Buddhaya
Namo Shakyamunaye Buddhaya (response) [BELL, BELL]
Namo Shakyamunaye Buddhaya
Namo Shakyamunaye Buddhaya (response) [BELL]

EVENING CHANT, *Version Two* ♪

With posture upright and stable, we are seated at the foot of the
Bodhi tree. [BELL]
Body, speech, and mind are one in stillness; there is no more
thought of right and wrong. [BELL]
Our mind and body dwell in perfect mindfulness.
We rediscover our original nature, leaving the shore of illusion behind.
[BELL]
Noble Sangha, diligently bring your mind into meditation.
Namo Shakyamunaye Buddhaya
Namo Shakyamunaye Buddhaya (response) [BELL]
Namo Shakyamunaye Buddhaya
Namo Shakyamunaye Buddhaya (response) [BELL, BELL]
Namo Shakyamunaye Buddhaya
Namo Shakyamunaye Buddhaya (response) [BELL]

At the end of the sitting meditation there is one sound of the bell and
people can slowly come out of their meditation, uncross their legs, and
massage their limbs gently.

Eating Meditation

ALTHOUGH A FORMAL MEAL can be silent from beginning to end, in our lives at home a meal can be partly silent. Just a few minutes silence at the beginning after reading the Five Contemplations may be enough, if you want the meal to be a time for the family to be together and share their happiness in words. Eating in silence allows us to see the preciousness of the food and our friends, and also our close relationship with the earth and all species. Every vegetable, every drop of water, every piece of bread contains in it the life of our whole planet and the sun. With each bite of food, we can taste the meaning and value of our life. We can meditate on the plants, on the work of the farmer and the cook that have brought this food to us. As we place food on our empty plate we can remember the many thousands of children who die each day for lack of food. Sitting silently at the table with others, we also have the opportunity to see each other clearly and deeply, and to smile to communicate real love and friendship.

As we eat we nourish our spirit as well as our body. This means that whatever we say or think during the meal should make it easy for the food to digest. We avoid saying or thinking what is negative. We say and think what brings happiness and love into the world. After we have finished eating we may want to sit with our family, our children, to hear them share about difficulties they may be going through.

The first time you eat in silence, it may seem awkward; but after you become used to it, silent meals can bring a great deal of peace, joy, and insight. These verses, recited silently to yourself, help you look deeply into all that is.

1. LOOKING AT YOUR EMPTY PLATE OR BOWL

My plate (bowl), empty now,
will soon be filled with precious food.
I see how fortunate I am
to have enough to eat
to continue the practice.

2. SERVING FOOD

In this food
I see clearly
the entire universe
supporting my existence.

3. SITTING DOWN TO BEGIN THE MEAL

Sitting here
is like sitting under a Bodhi tree.
My body is stable in mindfulness,
free from all distraction.

4. LOOKING AT THE PLATE OF FOOD BEFORE EATING

Beings all over the earth
are struggling to live.
I aspire to practice deeply
so that all may have enough to eat.

5. CONTEMPLATING THE FOOD

This plate of food,
so fragrant and appetizing,
also contains much suffering.

6. INTRODUCING THE FIVE CONTEMPLATIONS
[Read aloud by one person before beginning to eat]
[BELL, BELL, BELL]

The Buddha advises us to eat in mindfulness,
establishing ourselves in the present moment
so that we can be aware of the food and the community surrounding us.
Let us eat in a way that makes peace, joy, brotherhood, and sisterhood
possible during the whole time of eating.
Brothers and sisters, when you hear the bell, please meditate on the
Five Contemplations.
[BELL]

7. THE FIVE CONTEMPLATIONS
[Read aloud by one person before beginning to eat]

This food is a gift of the whole universe, numerous living beings,
and much hard and loving work.
May we eat with mindfulness and gratitude so as to be worthy
to receive it.
May we recognize and transform unwholesome mental formations, especially our greed.
May we keep our compassion alive by eating in such a way that we reduce the suffering of beings, stop contributing to climate degradation,
and heal and preserve our precious planet.
We accept this food so that we may nurture our sisterhood and brotherhood, build our Sangha, and realize our ideal of serving
all beings.
[BELL]

8. BEGINNING TO EAT
[Recited silently while chewing the first four mouthfuls]

I eat the first mouthful to bring joy to someone today.
I eat the second mouthful to relieve the suffering of someone today.
I eat the third mouthful to experience joy in my life.
I eat the fourth mouthful to love all beings equally.

9. WHEN THE PLATE OR BOWL IS EMPTY

My plate (bowl) is empty.
My hunger is satisfied.
I feel gratitude to my parents, teachers, friends, and all beings.

10. DRINKING TEA

This cup of tea in my two hands,
is mindfulness held perfectly.
My mind and body dwell
in the very here and now.

11. WASHING THE DISHES

Washing the dishes is like bathing a baby Buddha.
The profane is the sacred.
Everyday mind is Buddha's mind.

Deep Relaxation

[The following is an example of how to guide yourself or others in deep relaxation. Allowing your body to rest is very important. When your body is at ease and relaxed, your mind will be at peace as well. The practice of deep relaxation is essential for your body and mind to heal. Please take the time to practice it often. although the following guided relaxation may take you thirty minutes, feel free to modify it to fit your situation. Just ten minutes when you wake up in the morning, before going to bed in. the evening, or during a short break in the middle of a busy day will relax your body and mind.]

LIE DOWN comfortably with your back on a mat on the floor. It is important to be warm. You may need a blanket. Close your eyes. Allow your arms to rest gently on either side of your body and let your legs relax, turning your feet outwards.

As you breathe in and out, become aware of all the areas of your body that are touching the floor: your heels, the backs of your legs, your buttocks, your back, the backs of your hands and arms, the back of your head. With each out-breath, feel yourself sinking deeper and deeper into the floor, letting go of tension, letting go of worries, not holding on to anything.

As you breathe in, feel your abdomen rising; as your breathe out, feel your abdomen falling. For several breaths, just notice the rise and fall of your abdomen.

Now as you breathe in, become aware of your feet. As you breathe out, allow your feet to relax. Breathing in, send your love to your feet; breathing out, smile to your feet. As you breathe in and out, know how wonderful it is to have feet that allow you to walk, run, play sports, dance, drive, and do so many other activities throughout the day. Send your gratitude to your feet for always being there for you wherever you need them.

Breathing in, become aware of your right and left legs. Breathing out, allow all the cells in your legs to relax. Breathing in, smile to your legs; breathing out, send them your love. Appreciate whatever degree of strength and health is there in your legs. As you breathe in and out, send them your tenderness and care. Allow them to rest, sinking gently into the floor. Release any tension you may be holding in your legs.

Breathing in, become aware of your hands lying on the floor. Breathing out, completely relax all the muscles in your hands, releasing any tension you may be holding in them. As you breathe in, appreciate how wonderful it is to have hands. As you breathe out, send a smile of love to your hands. Breathe in and out and be in touch with all the things your hands allow you to do: cook, write, drive, hold someone's hand, hold a baby, wash your own body, draw, play a musical instrument, type, build and fix things, pet an animal, hold a cup of tea. So many things are available to you because of your hands. Just enjoy the fact that you have two hands, and allow all the cells in your hands to really rest.

Breathing in, become aware of your arms. Breathing out, let your arms fully relax. As you breathe in, send your love to your arms; as you breathe out, smile to them. Take the time to appreciate your arms and whatever strength and health are there in them. Send them your gratitude for allowing you to hug someone, to swing on a swing, to help and serve others, to work—cleaning the house, mowing the lawn, doing so many things throughout the day. Breathing in and out, allow your arms to let go and rest completely on the floor. Feel the tension leaving your arms. As you embrace them with your mindfulness, feel joy and ease in every part of your arms.

Breathing in, become aware of your shoulders. Breathing out, allow any tension in your shoulders to flow out into the floor. As you breathe in, send your love to your shoulders; as you breathe out, smile with gratitude to them. Breathing in and out, be aware that you may have allowed tension and stress to accumulate in your shoulders. With each exhalation, allow the tension to leave your shoulders, and feel them relaxing more and more deeply. Send them your tenderness and care, knowing that you do not want to put too much strain on them, you want to live in a way that will allow them to be relaxed and at ease.

Breathing in, become aware of your heart. Breathing out, allow your heart to rest. With your in-breath, send your love to your heart. With your out-breath, smile to your heart. As you breathe in and out, get in touch with how wonderful it is to have a heart still beating in your chest. Your heart allows your life to be possible, and it is always there for you, every minute of every day. It never takes a break. Your heart has been beating since you were a four-week-old fetus in your mother's womb. It is a marvelous organ that allows you to do everything you do throughout the day. Breathe in and know that your heart also loves you. Breathe out and commit to live in a way that will help your heart to function well. With each exhalation, feel your heart relaxing more and more. Allow each cell in your heart to smile with ease and joy.

Breathing in, become aware of your stomach and intestines. Breathing out, allow your stomach and intestines to relax. As you breathe in, send them your love and gratitude. As you breathe out, smile tenderly to them. Breathing in and out, know how essential these organs are to your health. Give them the chance to rest deeply. Each day they digest and assimilate the food you eat, giving you energy and strength. They need you to take the time to recognize and appreciate them. As you breathe in, feel your stomach and intestines relaxing and releasing all tension. As you breathe out, smile to your stomach and intestines.

Breathing in, become aware of your eyes. Breathing out, allow your eyes and the muscles around your eyes to relax. Breathing in, smile to your eyes; breathing out, send them your love. Allow your eyes to rest and sink into their sockets. As you breathe in and out, know how precious your two eyes are. They allow you to look into the eyes of someone, to see a beautiful sunset, to read and write, to move around with ease, to see a bird flying in the sky, to watch a movie—so many things are possible because of your two eyes. Take the time to appreciate the miraculous gift of sight, and allow your eyes to rest deeply.

[*Here you can continue to relax other areas of your body, using the same pattern as above.*]

Now, if there is a place in your body that is sick or in pain, take this time to become aware of it and send it your love. Breathing in, allow this area to rest; breathing out, smile to it with great tenderness and affection. Be aware that there are other parts of your body that are still strong and healthy. Allow these strong parts of your body to send their strength and energy to the weak or sick area. Feel the support, energy, and love of the rest of your body penetrating the weak area, soothing and healing it. Breathe in and affirm your own capacity to heal; breathe out and let go of the worry or fear you may be holding in your body. Breathing in and out, smile with love and confidence to the area of your body that is not well.

Breathing in, become aware of the whole of your body lying down. Breathing out, enjoy the sensation of your whole body lying down, very relaxed and calm. Smile to your whole body as you breathe in, and send your love and compassion to your whole body as you breathe out. Feel all the cells in your whole body smiling joyfully with you. Feel gratitude for all the cells in your whole body. Return to the gentle rise and fall of your abdomen.

[*If you are guiding other people, and if you are comfortable doing so, you can now sing a few relaxing songs or lullabies.*]

To end, slowly stretch and open your eyes. Take your time to get up mindfully and lightly. Practice to carry the calmness and attentiveness you have generated into your next activity, and throughout the day.

Hugging Meditation

HUGGING IS PART of our culture but we can also see it as a spiritual practice. When bidding someone farewell or greeting someone, we offer them a mindful hug. We can also practice hugging meditation after the Rose ceremony or a funeral ceremony to express our feeling of unity with each those who continue the deceased.

If you wish to hug someone, always ask first "May I give you a hug?" If the answer is positive, you can join your palms in respect to the other. Looking at the other person you open your arms and hold each other for at least three in- and out-breaths. There is no need to pat each other's back. You can stand perfectly still and feel deeply the presence of yourself and the other. You feel the warmth in your bodies that signifies you are both alive and you know that being together is a miracle that becomes part of eternity.

gathas related to ceremonies

ॐ

THESE SHORT VERSES are to help us practice mindfulness as we attend a ceremony. Gathas are short poems or verses we can recite to help us dwell in mindfulness during different activities. While reciting gathas, we become deeply aware of the action we are engaged in, and this helps us to perform that action with understanding and love. These verses can be memorized and repeated, written out and placed in key locations in your life where you will see them daily, or kept with you in a pocket or a bag for any time you need a little reminder to return to yourself.*

ENTERING THE MEDITATION HALL

Entering the meditation hall,
I see my true self.
As I sit down,
I vow to cut off all disturbances.

INVITING THE BELL, *Version One*

Body, speech, and mind in perfect oneness,
I send my heart along with the sound of the bell.
May the hearers awaken from forgetfulness
and transcend all anxiety and sorrow.

INVITING THE BELL, *Version Two*

May the sound of this bell penetrate deeply into the cosmos.
In even the darkest places, may living beings hear it clearly
so their suffering will cease,
understanding arises in their hearts,
and they can transcend the path of anxiety and sorrow.
Namo Shakyamunaye Buddhaya

*For a complete set of gathas see *Present Moment, Wonderful Moment*, Thich Nhat Hanh, Parallax Press, 2022.

LISTENING TO THE BELL, *Version One*

I listen. I listen.
This wonderful sound
brings me back to my true home.

LISTENING TO THE BELL, *Version Two*

Hearing the bell, I let go of all my afflictions.
My heart is calm, my sorrows ended.
I am no longer bound to anything.
I learn to listen to my suffering
and the suffering of the other person.
When understanding is born in me,
compassion is also born.

LIGHTING A CANDLE

Lighting this candle,
offering the light to countless buddhas,
the peace and joy I feel,
brighten the face of the earth.

SITTING DOWN

Sitting here
is like sitting under a Bodhi tree.
My body is mindfulness itself,
free from all distraction.

FINDING A STABLE SITTING POSTURE

In the lotus position,
the human flower blooms.
The udumbara flower is here,
offering its true fragrance.

CALMING BODY AND MIND

Breathing in, I calm my body.
Breathing out, I smile.
Dwelling in the present moment,
I know this is a wonderful moment.

BREATHING, *Version One*

Breathing in, I know I'm breathing in.
Breathing out, I know I'm breathing out.
As my in-breath grows deep,
my out-breath grows slow.
Breathing in, I feel calm,
breathing out, I feel at ease.
Breathing in, I smile,
breathing out, I release.
Dwelling in the present moment,
I know this is a wonderful moment.

BREATHING, *Version Two*

I have arrived, I am home
in the here, in the now.
I am solid. I am free
In the ultimate, I dwell.

BREATHING, *Version Three*

In, Out.
Deep, Slow.
Calm, Ease.
Smile, Release.
Present moment, Wonderful moment.

ADJUSTING MEDITATION POSTURE

Feelings come and go
like clouds in a windy sky.
Conscious breathing
is my anchor.

GREETING SOMEONE
[WITH PALMS JOINED]

A lotus for you,
a Buddha-to-be.

Ceremonies

Ceremony to Recite the Two Promises (for children) ﴾

[If there are adults and children practicing together, this ceremony can be inserted into the ceremony for reciting the Five Mindfulness Trainings, after the recitation of the Sutra of the Insight that Brings us to the Other Shore].

1. INTRODUCTORY WORDS

Today the community has gathered to recite the Two Promises. Young members of the community, please come forward. Upon hearing the sound of the bell, please touch the earth three times to show your gratitude to the Buddha, the Dharma, and the Sangha.

[BELL, BELL, BELL]

2. RECITATION OF THE TWO PROMISES

Young people, now we will recite the Two Promises that you have made with the Buddha, and yourself. Will the entire community please join the young people in reciting after me:

I vow to develop understanding, (*the community repeats*) in order to live peacefully (*the community repeats*) with people, animals, plants, and minerals (*the community repeats*).

This is the first promise you have made with the Buddha, our teacher. Have you tried to learn more about it and to keep your promise during the past two weeks?

[THREE BREATHS]
[BELL]

I vow to develop my compassion (*the community repeats*), in order to protect the lives (*the community repeats*) of people, animals, plants, and minerals (*the community repeats*).

This is the second promise you have made with the Buddha, our teacher. Have you tried to learn more about it and to keep your promise during the past two weeks?
[THREE BREATHS]
[BELL]

3. CONCLUDING WORDS

Young students of the Enlightened One, understanding and love are the two most important teachings you can learn. If we do not make the effort to be open, to understand the suffering of other people, we will not be able to love them and to live in harmony with them. We should also try to understand and protect the lives of animals, plants, and minerals and live in harmony with them. If we cannot understand, we cannot love. The Buddha teaches us to look at living beings with the eyes of love and understanding. Please learn to practice this teaching.

Young people, upon hearing the sound of the bell, please stand up and touch the earth three times to show your gratitude.
[BELL, BELL, BELL]

Ceremony to Recite
the Five Mindfulness Trainings ೧

1. SITTING MEDITATION (12 MINUTES)

2. INCENSE OFFERING ♪

[BELL, BELL, BELL]
In gratitude, we offer this incense
throughout space and time
to all buddhas and bodhisattvas.
May it be fragrant as earth herself,
reflecting careful efforts,
wholehearted awareness,
and the fruit of understanding
slowly ripening.
May we and all beings
be companions of buddhas and bodhisattvas.
May we awaken from forgetfulness
and realize our true home.
[BELL]

3. TOUCHING THE EARTH ♪

Introductory Verse
The one who bows and the one who is bowed to
are both, by nature, empty.
Therefore the communication between them
is inexpressibly perfect.
Our practice center is the net of Indra
reflecting all buddhas everywhere.
And with my person in front of each buddha,
I go with my whole life for refuge.
[BELL]

Touching the Earth
[*Touch the earth one time at the sound of each bell.*]
Offering light in the ten directions,
the Buddha, the Dharma, and the Sangha,
to whom we bow in gratitude.
[BELL]

Teaching and living the way of awareness
in the very midst of suffering and confusion,
Shakyamuni Buddha, the Fully Enlightened One,
to whom we bow in gratitude.
[BELL]

Cutting through ignorance, awakening our hearts and our minds,
Manjushri, the Bodhisattva of Great Understanding,
to whom we bow in gratitude.
[BELL]

Working mindfully, working joyfully for the sake of all beings,
Samantabhadra, the Bodhisattva of Great Action,
to whom we bow in gratitude.
[BELL]

Listening deeply, serving beings in countless ways,
Avalokiteshvara, the Bodhisattva of Great Compassion,
to whom we bow in gratitude.
[BELL]

Fearless and persevering through realms of suffering and darkness,
Kshitigarbha, the Bodhisattva of Great Aspiration,
to whom we bow in gratitude.
[BELL]

Mother of buddhas, bodhisattvas, and all beings, nourishing,
holding, and healing all, Bodhisattva Gaia, Great Mother Earth,
precious jewel of the cosmos, to whom we bow in gratitude.
[BELL]

Radiating light in all directions, source of life on earth,
Mahavairocana Tathagata, Great Father Sun, Buddha of Infinite
Light and Life, to whom we bow in gratitude.
[BELL]

Showing the way fearlessly and compassionately,
the stream of all our ancestral teachers,
to whom we bow in gratitude.
[BELL, BELL]

4. Opening Verse ♪

[BELL, BELL, BELL]

Namo Tassa Bhagavato Arahato Samma Sambuddhassa
Namo Tassa Bhagavato Arahato Samma Sambuddhassa
Namo Tassa Bhagavato Arahato Samma Sambuddhassa
[BELL]

The Dharma is deep and lovely.
We now have a chance to see, study, and practice it.
We vow to realize its true meaning.
[BELL]

5. The Sutra of the Insight that Brings Us to the Other Shore

Avalokiteshvara, while practicing deeply
with the insight that brings us to the other shore,
suddenly discovered that all of the five skandhas are equally empty,
and with this realization he overcame all ill-being. [BELL]
"Listen Shariputra, this body itself is emptiness
and emptiness itself is this body.
This body is not other than emptiness
and emptiness is not other than this body.
The same is true of feelings, perceptions,
mental formations, and consciousness. [BELL]

"Listen Shariputra, all phenomena bear the mark of emptiness;
their true nature is the nature of no birth no death,

no being no nonbeing, no defilement no purity,
no increasing no decreasing. [BELL]

"That is why in emptiness, body, feelings,
perceptions, mental formations, and consciousness
are not separate self-entities.
The eighteen realms of phenomena, which are the six sense organs,
six sense objects, and six consciousnesses
are also not separate self-entities.
The Twelve Links of Interdependent Arising
and their extinction are also not separate self-entities.
Ill-being, the causes of ill-being,
the end of ill-being, the path, insight, and attainment,
are also not separate self-entities.
Whoever can see this
no longer needs anything to attain. [BELL]

"Bodhisattvas who practice the insight that brings us to the
other shore
see no more obstacles in their mind,
and because there are no more obstacles in their mind,
they can overcome all fear, destroy all wrong perceptions,
and realize perfect nirvana. [BELL]

"All buddhas in the past, present, and future
by practicing the insight that brings us to the other shore
are all capable of attaining authentic and perfect
enlightenment. [BELL]

"Therefore Shariputra, it should be known that
the insight that brings us to the other shore is a great mantra,
the most illuminating mantra, the highest mantra,
a mantra beyond compare,
the true wisdom that has the power
to put an end to all kinds of suffering. [BELL]

"Therefore let us proclaim a mantra
to praise the insight that brings us to the other shore
Gate gate paragate parasamgate bodhi svaha!

Gate gate paragate parasamgate bodhi svaha!
Gate gate paragate parasamgate bodhi svaha!"
[BELL BELL]

6. SANGHAKARMAN PROCEDURE*

Sanghakarman Master: Has the entire community assembled?
Sangha Convener: The entire community has assembled.
Sanghakarman Master: Is there harmony in the community?
Sangha Convener: Yes, there is harmony.
Sanghakarman Master: Is there anyone not able to be present who has asked to be represented, and have they declared themselves to have done their best to study and practice the Five Mindfulness Trainings?
Sangha Convener: No, there is not.
    or
Sangha Convener: Yes, [name], for health reasons, cannot be at the recitation today. They have asked [name] to represent them and they declare that they have done their best to study and practice the mindfulness trainings.
Sanghakarman Master: What is the reason for the community gathering today?
Sangha Convener: The community has gathered to practice the recitation of the Five Mindfulness Trainings.
Sanghakarman Master: Noble community, please listen. Today, [date], has been declared to be the Mindfulness Training Recitation Day. We have gathered at the appointed time. The noble community is ready to hear and recite the mindfulness trainings in an atmosphere of harmony, and the recitation can proceed. Is the sanghakarman procedure clear and complete?
Everyone: Clear and complete.
[BELL]

7. INTRODUCTORY WORDS

Dear Sangha, this is the moment when we enjoy reciting the Five Mindfulness Trainings together. The Five Mindfulness Trainings represent the

---

*The recitation of the Five Mindfulness Trainings should be done when the community is in harmony. The practice of Beginning Anew will help the community resolve conflicts.

Buddhist vision for a global spirituality and ethic. They are a concrete expression of the Buddha's teachings on the Four Noble Truths and the Noble Eightfold Path, the path of right understanding and true love, leading to healing, transformation, and happiness for ourselves and for the world. To practice the Five Mindfulness Trainings is to cultivate the insight of interbeing, or Right View, which can remove all discrimination, intolerance, anger, fear, and despair. If we live according to the Five Mindfulness Trainings, we are already on the path of a bodhisattva. Knowing we are on that path, we are not lost in confusion about our life in the present or in fears about the future.

Please listen to each mindfulness training with a serene mind. Breathe mindfully and answer "yes" silently every time you see that you have made an effort to study, practice, and observe the mindfulness training read.

8. RECITING THE FIVE MINDFULNESS TRAININGS

The First Mindfulness Training: Reverence for Life

Aware of the suffering caused by the destruction of life, I am committed to cultivating the insight of interbeing and compassion and learning ways to protect the lives of people, animals, plants, and minerals. I am determined not to kill, not to let others kill, and not to support any act of killing in the world, in my thinking, or in my way of life. Seeing that harmful actions arise from anger, fear, greed, and intolerance, which in turn come from dualistic and discriminative thinking, I will cultivate openness, nondiscrimination, and nonattachment to views in order to transform violence, fanaticism, and dogmatism in myself and in the world.

This is the first of the Five Mindfulness Trainings. Have we made an effort to study, practice, and observe it during the past two weeks?
[Three breaths]
[BELL]*

The Second Mindfulness Training: True Happiness

Aware of the suffering caused by exploitation, social injustice, stealing, and oppression, I am committed to practicing generosity in my thinking,

---

*When the bell master wishes the reader to proceed with the next training, they stop the sound of the bell by placing the inviter against the rim.

speaking, and acting. I am determined not to steal and not to possess anything that should belong to others; and I will share my time, energy, and material resources with those who are in need. I will practice looking deeply to see that the happiness and suffering of others are not separate from my own happiness and suffering; that true happiness is not possible without understanding and compassion; and that running after wealth, fame, power, and sensual pleasures can bring much suffering and despair. I am aware that happiness depends on my mental attitude and not on external conditions, and that I can live happily in the present moment simply by remembering that I already have more than enough conditions to be happy. I am committed to practicing Right Livelihood so that I can help reduce the suffering of living beings on earth and reverse the process of global warming.

This is the second of the Five Mindfulness Trainings. Have we made an effort to study, practice, and observe it during the past two weeks?
[*Three breaths*]
[BELL]

The Third Mindfulness Training: True Love

Aware of the suffering caused by sexual misconduct, I am committed to cultivating responsibility and learning ways to protect the safety and integrity of individuals, couples, families, and society. Knowing that sexual desire is not love, and that sexual activity motivated by craving always harms myself as well as others, I am determined not to engage in sexual relations without mutual consent, true love, and a deep, long-term commitment. I resolve to find spiritual support for the integrity of my relationship from family members, friends, and sangha with whom there is support and trust. I will do everything in my power to protect children from sexual abuse and to prevent couples and families from being broken by sexual misconduct. Seeing that body and mind are interrelated, I am committed to learn appropriate ways to take care of my sexual energy and to cultivate the four basic elements of true love—loving kindness, compassion, joy, and inclusiveness—for the greater happiness of myself and others. Recognizing the diversity of human experience, I am committed not to discriminate against any form of gender identity or sexual orientation. Practicing true love, we know that we will continue beautifully into the future.

This is the third of the Five Mindfulness Trainings. Have we made an effort to study, practice, and observe it during the past two weeks?
[*Three breaths*]
[BELL]

The Fourth Mindfulness Training: Loving Speech and Deep Listening

Aware of the suffering caused by unmindful speech and the inability to listen to others, I am committed to cultivating loving speech and compassionate listening in order to relieve suffering and to promote reconciliation and peace in myself and among other people, ethnic and religious groups, and nations. Knowing that words can create happiness or suffering, I am committed to speaking truthfully using words that inspire confidence, joy, and hope. When anger is manifesting in me, I am determined not to speak. I will practice mindful breathing and walking in order to recognize and to look deeply into my anger. I know that the roots of anger can be found in my wrong perceptions and lack of understanding of the suffering in myself and in the other person. I will speak and listen in a way that can help myself and the other person to transform suffering and see the way out of difficult situations. I am determined not to spread news that I do not know to be certain and not to utter words that can cause division or discord. I will practice Right Diligence to nourish my capacity for understanding, love, joy, and inclusiveness, and gradually transform anger, violence, and fear that lie deep in my consciousness.

This is the fourth of the Five Mindfulness Trainings. Have we made an effort to study, practice, and observe it during the past two weeks?
[*Three breaths*]
[BELL]

The Fifth Mindfulness Training: Nourishment and Healing

Aware of the suffering caused by unmindful consumption, I am committed to cultivating good health, both physical and mental, for myself, my family, and my society by practicing mindful eating, drinking, and consuming. I will practice looking deeply into how I consume the Four Kinds of Nutriments, namely edible foods, sense impressions, volition, and consciousness. I am determined not to gamble, or to use alcohol, drugs, or any other products which contain toxins, such as certain websites, electronic games, TV programs, films, magazines, books, and conversations. I will practice coming back to the present moment to be in touch with the refreshing, healing and nourishing elements in me and around me, not letting regrets and sorrow drag me back into the past nor letting anxieties, fear, or craving pull me out of the present moment. I am determined not to try to cover up loneliness, anxiety, or other suffering by losing myself in consumption. I will contemplate interbeing and consume in a way that preserves peace, joy, and well-being in my body and consciousness, and in the collective body and consciousness of my family, my society, and the earth.

This is the fifth of the Five Mindfulness Trainings. Have we made an effort to study, practice, and observe it during the past two weeks?
[*Three breaths*]
[BELL]

9. CONCLUDING WORDS

Brothers and sisters, we have recited the Five Mindfulness Trainings, the foundation of happiness for the individual, the family, and society. We should recite them regularly so that our study and practice of the mindfulness trainings can deepen day by day.

Upon hearing the sound of the bell, let us stand up and touch the earth three times to show your gratitude to the Buddha, the Dharma, and the Sangha.
[BELL, BELL, BELL]

10. SHARING THE MERIT ♪

Reciting the trainings, practicing the way of awareness
gives rise to benefits without limit.
We vow to share the fruits with all beings.
We vow to offer tribute to parents, teachers, friends, and numerous beings
who give guidance and support along the path.
[BELL, BELL, BELL]

Ceremony to Recite the Fourteen Mindfulness Trainings ॐ

1. SITTING MEDITATION [12 MINUTES]

2. INCENSE OFFERING ♪

[BELL, BELL, BELL]
In gratitude, we offer this incense
throughout space and time
to all buddhas and bodhisattvas.
May it be fragrant as earth herself,
reflecting careful efforts,
wholehearted awareness,
and the fruit of understanding
slowly ripening.
May we and all beings
be companions of buddhas and bodhisattvas.
May we awaken from forgetfulness
and realize our true home.
[BELL]

3. TOUCHING THE EARTH ♪

Introductory Verse
The one who bows and the one who is bowed to
are both, by nature, empty.
Therefore the communication between them
is inexpressibly perfect.
Our practice center is the net of Indra
reflecting all buddhas everywhere.
And with my person in front of each buddha,
I go with my whole life for refuge.
[BELL]

Touching the Earth
[*Touch the earth one time at the sound of each bell.*]

Offering light in the ten directions,
the Buddha, the Dharma, and the Sangha,
to whom we bow in gratitude.
[BELL]

Teaching and living the way of awareness
in the very midst of suffering and confusion,
Shakyamuni Buddha, the Fully Enlightened One,
to whom we bow in gratitude.
[BELL]

Cutting through ignorance, awakening our hearts and our minds,
Manjushri, the Bodhisattva of Great Understanding,
to whom we bow in gratitude.
[BELL]

Working mindfully, working joyfully for the sake of all beings,
Samantabhadra, the Bodhisattva of Great Action,
to whom we bow in gratitude.
[BELL]

Listening deeply, serving beings in countless ways,
Avalokiteshvara, the Bodhisattva of Great Compassion,
to whom we bow in gratitude.
[BELL]

Fearless and persevering through realms of suffering and darkness,
Kshitigarbha, the Bodhisattva of Great Aspiration,
to whom we bow in gratitude.
[BELL]

Mother of buddhas, bodhisattvas, and all beings, nourishing,
holding, and healing all, Bodhisattva Gaia, Great Mother Earth,
precious jewel of the cosmos, to whom we bow in gratitude.
[BELL]

Radiating light in all directions, source of life on earth,
Mahavairocana Tathagata, Great Father Sun, Buddha of Infinite
Light and Life, to whom we bow in gratitude.
[BELL]

Showing the way fearlessly and compassionately,
the stream of all our ancestral teachers,
to whom we bow in gratitude.
[BELL, BELL]

4. OPENING VERSE ♪
[BELL, BELL, BELL]

Namo Tassa Bhagavato Arahato Samma Sambuddhassa
Namo Tassa Bhagavato Arahato Samma Sambuddhassa
Namo Tassa Bhagavato Arahato Samma Sambuddhassa
[BELL]

The Dharma is deep and lovely.
We now have a chance to see, study, and practice it.
We vow to realize its true meaning.
[BELL]

5. THE SUTRA OF THE INSIGHT THAT BRINGS US TO THE OTHER SHORE ♪

Avalokiteshvara, while practicing deeply
with the insight that brings us to the other shore,
suddenly discovered that all of the five skandhas are equally empty,
and with this realization he overcame all ill-being. [BELL]
"Listen Shariputra, this body itself is emptiness
and emptiness itself is this body.
This body is not other than emptiness
and emptiness is not other than this body.
The same is true of feelings, perceptions,
mental formations, and consciousness. [BELL]

"Listen Shariputra, all phenomena bear the mark of emptiness;
their true nature is the nature of no birth no death,

no being no nonbeing, no defilement no purity,
no increasing no decreasing. [BELL]

"That is why in emptiness, body, feelings,
perceptions, mental formations, and consciousness
are not separate self-entities.
The eighteen realms of phenomena, which are the six sense organs,
six sense objects, and six consciousnesses
are also not separate self-entities.
The Twelve Links of Interdependent Arising
and their extinction are also not separate self-entities.
Ill-being, the causes of ill-being,
the end of ill-being, the path, insight, and attainment,
are also not separate self-entities.
Whoever can see this
no longer needs anything to attain. [BELL]

"Bodhisattvas who practice the insight that brings us to the
other shore
see no more obstacles in their mind,
and because there are no more obstacles in their mind,
they can overcome all fear, destroy all wrong perceptions,
and realize perfect nirvana. [BELL]

"All buddhas in the past, present, and future
by practicing the insight that brings us to the other shore
are all capable of attaining authentic and perfect
enlightenment. [BELL]

"Therefore Shariputra, it should be known that
the insight that brings us to the other shore is a great mantra,
the most illuminating mantra, the highest mantra,
a mantra beyond compare,
the true wisdom that has the power
to put an end to all kinds of suffering. [BELL]

"Therefore let us proclaim a mantra
to praise the insight that brings us to the other shore
Gate gate paragate parasamgate bodhi svaha!
[BELL, BELL]

6. SANGHAKARMAN PROCEDURE

Sanghakarman Master: Has the entire community assembled?

Sangha Convener: The entire community has assembled.

Sanghakarman Master: Is there harmony in the community?

Sangha Convener: Yes, there is harmony.

Sanghakarman Master: Is there anyone not able to be present who has asked to be represented, and have they declared themselves to have done their best to study and practice the mindfulness trainings?

Sangha Convener: No, there is not.

or

Sangha Convener: Yes, order member [name], for health reasons, cannot be at the recitation today. They have asked order member [name], to represent them, and they declare that they have done their best to study and practice the mindfulness trainings.

Sanghakarman Master: Why has the community assembled today?

Sangha Convener: The community has assembled to practice the recitation of the Fourteen Mindfulness Trainings of the Order of Interbeing.

Sanghakarman Master: Noble community, please listen. Today, [date], has been declared as the day to recite the Fourteen Mindfulness Trainings of the Order of Interbeing. The community has assembled at the appointed time and is ready to hear and to recite the Fourteen Mindfulness Trainings in an atmosphere of harmony. Thus, the recitation can proceed. Is the sanghakarman procedure clear and complete?

Everyone: Clear and complete.

[BELL]

7. RECITING THE FOURTEEN MINDFULNESS TRAININGS OF THE ORDER OF INTERBEING

Dear Sangha, this is the moment when we enjoy reciting the Fourteen Mindfulness Trainings of the Order of Interbeing. The Fourteen Mindfulness Trainings are the very essence of the Order of Interbeing. They are the torch lighting our path, the boat carrying us, the teacher guiding us. They allow us to touch the nature of interbeing in everything that is, and to see that our happiness is not separate from the happiness of others. Interbeing is not a theory; it is a reality that can be directly experienced by each of us at any moment in our daily lives. The Fourteen Mindfulness Trainings help us cultivate concentration and insight which free us from fear and the illusion of a separate self.

Please listen to each Mindfulness Training with a serene mind. The mindfulness trainings serve as a clear mirror in which to look at ourselves. Say yes, silently, every time you see that you have made and effort to study, practice and observe the mindfulness training read.

The First Mindfulness Training: Openness

Aware of the suffering created by fanaticism and intolerance, we are determined not to be idolatrous about or bound to any doctrine, theory, or ideology, even Buddhist ones. We are committed to seeing the Buddhist teachings as a guiding means that help us learn to look deeply and develop understanding and compassion. They are not doctrines to fight, kill, or die for. We understand that fanaticism in its many forms is the result of perceiving things in a dualistic or discriminative manner. We will train ourselves to look at everything with openness and the insight of interbeing in order to transform dogmatism and violence in ourselves and the world.

This is the First Mindfulness Training of the Order of Interbeing. Have we made an effort to study, practice, and observe it during the past two weeks? [*Three breaths*]
[BELL]

The Second Mindfulness Training: Nonattachment to Views

Aware of the suffering created by attachment to views and wrong perceptions, we are determined to avoid being narrow-minded and bound to present views. We are committed to learning and practicing nonattachment from views and being open to others' insights and experiences in order to benefit from the collective wisdom. Insight is revealed through the practice of compassionate listening, deep looking, and letting go of notions rather than through the accumulation of intellectual knowledge. We are aware that the knowledge we presently possess is not changeless, absolute truth. Truth is found in life, and we will observe life within and around us in every moment, ready to learn throughout our lives.

This is the Second Mindfulness Training of the Order of Interbeing. Have we made an effort to study, practice, and observe it during the past two weeks?
[*Three breaths*]
[BELL]

The Third Mindfulness Training: Freedom of Thought

Aware of the suffering brought about when we impose our view on others, we are determined not to force others, even our children, by any means whatsoever—such as authority, threat, money, propaganda, or indoctrination—to adopt our views. We are committed to respecting the rights of others to be different, to choose what to believe and how to decide. We will, however, learn to help others let go of and transform narrowness through loving speech and compassionate dialogue.

This is the Third Mindfulness Training of the Order of Interbeing. Have we made an effort to study, practice, and observe it during the past two weeks?
[*Three breaths*]
[BELL]

The Fourth Mindfulness Training: Awareness of Suffering

Aware that looking deeply at the nature of suffering can help us cultivate understanding and compassion, we are determined to come home to ourselves, to recognize, accept, embrace, and listen to our own suffering with the energy of mindfulness. We will do our best not to run away from our suffering or cover it up through consumption but practice conscious breathing and walking to look deeply into the roots of our suffering. We know we can only find the path leading to the transformation of suffering when we understand the roots of suffering. Once we have understood our own suffering, we will be able to understand the suffering of others. We are committed to finding ways, including personal contact and using the telephone, electronic, audiovisual, and other means to be with those who suffer, so we can help them transform their suffering into compassion, peace, and joy.

This is the Fourth Mindfulness Training of the Order of Interbeing. Have we made an effort to study, practice, and observe it during the past two weeks?
[*Three breaths*]
[BELL]

The Fifth Mindfulness Training: Compassionate, Healthy Living

Aware that happiness is rooted in peace, solidity, freedom, and compassion, we are determined not to accumulate wealth while millions are hungry and dying nor to take as the aim of our life fame, profit, wealth, or sensual pleasure, which can bring much suffering and despair. We will practice looking deeply into how we nourish our body and mind with edible foods, sense impressions, volition, and consciousness. We are committed not to gamble or to use alcohol, drugs or any other products that bring toxins into our own and the collective body and consciousness such as certain websites, electronic games, TV programs, films, magazines, books, and conversations. We will consume in a way that preserves compassion, peace, joy, and well-being in our bodies and consciousness and in the collective body and consciousness of our families, our society, and the earth.

This is the Fifth Mindfulness Training of the Order of Interbeing. Have we made an effort to study, practice, and observe it during the past two weeks?
[*Three breaths*]
[BELL]

The Sixth Mindfulness Training: Taking Care of Anger
Aware that anger blocks communication and creates suffering, we are committed to taking care of our energy of anger when it arises, to recognizing and transforming the seeds of anger that lie deep in our consciousness. When anger manifests, we are determined not to do or say anything, but to practice mindful breathing or mindful walking to acknowledge, embrace, and look deeply into our anger. We know that the roots of anger are not outside of ourselves but can be found in our wrong perceptions and lack of understanding of the suffering in ourselves and the other person. By contemplating impermanence, we will be able to look with the eyes of compassion at ourselves and those we think are the cause of our anger, and to recognize the preciousness of our relationships. We will practice Right Diligence in order to nourish our capacity of understanding, love, joy, and inclusiveness, gradually transforming our anger, violence, and fear and helping others do the same.

This is the Sixth Mindfulness Training of the Order of Interbeing. Have we made an effort to study, practice, and observe it during the past two weeks?
[*Three breaths*]
[BELL]

The Seventh Mindfulness Training:
Dwelling Happily in the Present Moment
Aware that life is available only in the present moment, we are committed to training ourselves to live deeply each moment of daily life. We will try not to lose ourselves in dispersion or be carried away by regrets about the past, worries about the future, or cravings, anger, or jealousy in the present. We will practice mindful breathing to be aware of what is happening in the here and now. We are determined to learn the art of mindful living by touching the wondrous, refreshing, and healing elements that are inside and around us, in all situations. In this way, we will be able to cultivate seeds of joy, peace, love, and understanding in ourselves, thus facilitating the work of transformation and healing in our consciousness. We are aware that happiness depends primarily on our mental attitude and not on external conditions, and that we can live happily in the present moment simply by remembering that we already have more than enough conditions to be happy.

This is the Seventh Mindfulness Training of the Order of Interbeing. Have we made an effort to study, practice, and observe it during the past two weeks?
[*Three breaths*]
[BELL]

The Eighth Mindfulness Training: True Community and Communication
Aware that lack of communication always brings separation and suffering, we are committed to training ourselves in the practice of compassionate listening and loving speech. Knowing that true community is rooted in inclusiveness and in the concrete practice of harmony of views, thinking, and speech, we will practice to share our understanding and experiences with members in our community in order to arrive at collective insight. We are determined to learn to listen deeply without judging or reacting, and refrain from uttering words that can create discord or cause the community to break. Whenever difficulties arise, we will remain in our Sangha and practice looking deeply into ourselves and others to recognize all the causes and conditions, including our own habit energies, that have brought about the difficulties. We will take responsibility for all the ways we may have contributed to the conflict and keep communication open. We will not behave as a victim but be active in finding ways to reconcile and resolve all conflicts however small.

This is the Eighth Mindfulness Training of the Order of Interbeing. Have we made an effort to study, practice, and observe it during the past two weeks?
[*Three breaths*]
[BELL]

The Ninth Mindfulness Training: Truthful and Loving Speech

Aware that words can create happiness or suffering, we are committed to learning to speak truthfully, lovingly, and constructively. We will only use words that inspire joy, confidence, and hope as well as promote reconciliation and peace in ourselves and among people. We will speak and listen in a way that can help ourselves and others to transform suffering and see the way out of difficult situations. We are determined not to say untruthful things for the sake of personal interest or to impress people, nor to utter words that might cause division or hatred. We will protect the joy and harmony of our sangha by refraining from speaking about the faults of another person in their absence and always ask ourselves whether our perceptions are correct. We will speak only with the intention to understand and help transform the situation. We will not spread rumors nor criticize or condemn things of which we are not sure. We will do our best to speak out about situations of injustice, even when doing so may make difficulties for us or threaten our safety.

This is the Ninth Mindfulness Training of the Order of Interbeing. Have we made an effort to study, practice, and observe it during the past two weeks?
[*Three breaths*]
[BELL]

The Tenth Mindfulness Training: Protecting and Nourishing the Sangha

Aware that the essence and aim of a sangha is the practice of understanding and compassion, we are determined not to use the Buddhist community for personal power or profit or transform our community into a political instrument. However, as members of a spiritual community, we should take a clear stand against oppression and injustice. We should strive to change the situation, without taking sides in a conflict. We are committed to looking with the eyes of interbeing and learning to see ourselves and others as cells in one sangha body. As a true cell in the sangha body, generating mindfulness, concentration, and insight to nourish ourselves and the whole community, each of us is at the same time a cell in the Buddha body. We will actively build brotherhood and sisterhood, flow as a river, and practice to develop the three real powers—love, understanding, and cutting through afflictions—to realize collective awakening.

This is the Tenth Mindfulness Training of the Order of Interbeing. Have we made an effort to study, practice, and observe it during the past two weeks?
[*Three breaths*]
[BELL]

The Eleventh Mindfulness Training: Right Livelihood
Aware that great violence and injustice have been done to our environment and society, we are committed not to live with a vocation that is harmful to humans or nature. We will do our best to select a livelihood that contributes to the well-being of all species on earth and helps realize our ideal of understanding and compassion. Aware of economic, political, and social realities around the world, as well as our interrelationship with the ecosystem, we are determined to behave responsibly as consumers and citizens. We will not invest in or purchase from companies that contribute to the depletion of natural resources, harm the earth, and deprive others of the chance to live.

This is the Eleventh Mindfulness Training of the Order of Interbeing. Have we made an effort to study, practice, and observe it during the past two weeks?
[*Three breaths*]
[BELL]

The Twelfth Mindfulness Training: Reverence for Life
Aware that much suffering is caused by war and conflict, we are determined to cultivate nonviolence, compassion, and the insight of interbeing in our daily lives and promote peace education, mindful mediation, and reconciliation within families, communities, ethnic and religious groups, nations, and in the world. We are committed not to kill and not to let others kill. We will not support any act of killing in the world, in our thinking or in our way of life. We will diligently practice deep looking with our Sangha to discover better ways to protect life, prevent war, and build peace.

This is the Twelfth Mindfulness Training of the Order of Interbeing. Have we made an effort to study, practice, and observe it during the past two weeks?
[*Three breaths*]
[BELL]

The Thirteenth Mindfulness Training: Generosity

Aware of the suffering caused by exploitation, social injustice, stealing, and oppression, we are committed to cultivating generosity in our way of thinking, speaking, and acting. We will learn better ways to work for the well-being of people, animals, plants, and minerals and will practice generosity by sharing our time, energy, and material resources with those who are in need. We are determined not to steal and not to possess anything that should belong to others. We will respect the property of others, but will try to prevent others from profiting from human suffering or the suffering of other beings.

This is the Thirteenth Mindfulness Training of the Order of Interbeing. Have we made an effort to study, practice, and observe it during the past two weeks?
[*Three breaths*]
[BELL]

The Fourteenth Mindfulness Training: True Love

[*For lay members*]: Aware that sexual desire is not love and that sexual relations motivated by craving cannot dissipate the feeling of loneliness but will create more suffering, frustration, and isolation, we are determined not to engage in sexual relations without mutual understanding, love, and a deep long-term commitment. We resolve to find spiritual support for the integrity of our relationships from family members, friends, and sangha with whom there is support and trust. We know that to preserve the happiness of ourselves and others, we must respect the rights and commitments of ourselves and others. Recognizing the diversity of human experience, we are committed not to discriminate against any form of gender identity or sexual orientation. Seeing that body and mind are interrelated, we are committed to learning appropriate ways to take care of our sexual energy and cultivating loving kindness, compassion, joy, and inclusiveness for our own happiness and the happiness of others. We must be aware of future suffering that may be caused by sexual relations. We will treat our bodies with compassion and respect. We are determined to look deeply into the Four Nutriments and learn ways to preserve and channel our vital energies (sexual, breath, spirit) for the realization of our bodhisattva ideal. We will do everything in our power to protect children from sexual abuse and to protect couples and families from being broken by sexual misconduct. We will be fully aware of the responsibility of bringing new lives into the world, and will meditate regularly upon their future environment.

[*For monastic members*]: Aware that the deep aspiration of a monk or a nun can only be realized when he or she wholly leaves behind the bonds of sensual love, we are committed to practicing chastity and to helping others protect themselves. We are aware that loneliness and suffering cannot be alleviated through a sexual relationship, but through practicing loving kindness, compassion, joy, and inclusiveness. We know that a sexual relationship will destroy our monastic life, will prevent us from realizing our ideal of serving living beings, and will harm others. We will learn appropriate ways to take care of sexual energy. We are determined not to suppress or mistreat our body or to look upon our body as only an instrument, but to learn to handle our body with compassion and respect. We are determined to look deeply into the Four Nutriments in order to preserve and channel our vital energies (sexual, breath, spirit) for the realization of our bodhisattva ideal.

This is the Fourteenth Mindfulness Training of the Order of Interbeing. Have we made an effort to study, practice, and observe it during the past two weeks?
[*Three breaths*]
[BELL]

8. CONCLUDING WORDS

Brothers and sisters, I have recited the Fourteen Mindfulness Trainings of the Order of Interbeing as the community has wished. I thank all my sisters and brothers for helping me do it serenely.

9. SHARING THE MERIT ♪

Reciting the trainings, practicing the way of awareness
gives rise to benefits without limit.
We vow to share the fruits with all beings.
We vow to offer tribute to parents, teachers, friends,
and numerous beings
who give guidance and support along the path.
[BELL, BELL, BELL]

Ceremony to Transmit the Two Promises (for children) ॐ

1. INTRODUCTORY WORDS

Today the community has gathered to give support to the young people who will make the two promises. Will the entire community please enjoy your breathing and remain mindful when you hear the three sounds of the bell. The sound of the bell is the voice of the Buddha, bringing us back to our true home.
[BELL, BELL, BELL]

Dear young people you can make this promise with the Buddha-seed in yourself. The Two Promises will help you be aware of the suffering and the happiness of people, animals, plants, and minerals. You will be able to look after and preserve this planet Earth. Will the entire community please join the young people in repeating after me:

2. TRANSMISSION OF THE TWO PROMISES

Here is the first Promise:
I vow to develop understanding (*repeat*)
in order to live peacefully (*repeat*)
with people, animals, plants, and minerals. (*repeat*)

This is the first Promise. Do you promise to the Buddha-seed within you that you will do your best to practice it?
[THREE BREATHS]
[BELL]

Here is the second Promise:
I vow to develop my compassion (*repeat*)
in order to protect the lives (*repeat*)
of people, animals, plants, and minerals. (*repeat*)

This is the second Promise. Do you promise to the Buddha-seed within you that you will do your best to practice it?

[THREE BREATHS]

[BELL]

3. CONCLUDING WORDS

Young students of the Enlightened One, understanding and love are the two most important teachings of the Buddha. If we try to be open and to understand the difficulties of other people, we will be able to love them and to live in harmony with them. The same is true for animals, plants, and minerals. If we cannot understand others, then we cannot love. The Buddha teaches us to look at living beings with the eyes of love and understanding. Please learn to practice this teaching.

Young people, upon hearing the sound of the bell, please stand up and touch the earth three times to the Three Jewels, and then, you can go back to your seat.

[The young people touch the earth one time at the sound of each bell]

[BELL, BELL, BELL]

4. READING THE TWO PROMISES CERTIFICATE

[The transmitter reads the certificate on which are written the Two Promises, the Dharma name of the child, and the name of his or her teacher. Then the certificate is given to the young person.]

Dear young people, I will now read the Two Promises Certificate. When you hear your name, please come forward to receive your certificate.

5. SHARING THE MERIT ♪

Reciting the trainings, practicing the way of awareness
gives rise to benefits without limit.
We vow to share the fruits with all beings.
We vow to offer tribute to parents, teachers, friends,
and numerous beings
who give guidance and support along the path.

[BELL, BELL, BELL]

Ceremony to Transmit the Five Mindfulness Trainings ॐ

[This ceremony must be presided over by at least one Dharma teachers who has received the lamp in the Plum Village tradition.]

1. SITTING MEDITATION [12 MINUTES]

2. INCENSE OFFERING ♪

[BELL, BELL, BELL]
In gratitude, we offer this incense
throughout space and time
to all buddhas and bodhisattvas.
May it be fragrant as earth herself,
reflecting careful efforts,
wholehearted awareness,
and the fruit of understanding
slowly ripening.
May we and all beings
be companions of buddhas and bodhisattvas.
May we awaken from forgetfulness
and realize our true home.
[BELL]

3. TOUCHING THE EARTH ♪

Introductory Verse
The one who bows and the one who is bowed to
are both, by nature, empty.
Therefore the communication between them
is inexpressibly perfect.
Our practice center is the net of Indra
reflecting all buddhas everywhere.
And with my person in front of each buddha,
I go with my whole life for refuge.
[BELL]

Touching the Earth
[Touch the earth one time at the sound of each bell.]
Offering light in the ten directions,
the Buddha, the Dharma, and the Sangha,
to whom we bow in gratitude.
[BELL]

Teaching and living the way of awareness
in the very midst of suffering and confusion,
Shakyamuni Buddha, the Fully Enlightened One,
to whom we bow in gratitude.
[BELL]

Cutting through ignorance, awakening our hearts and our minds,
Manjushri, the Bodhisattva of Great Understanding,
to whom we bow in gratitude.
[BELL]

Working mindfully, working joyfully for the sake of all beings,
Samantabhadra, the Bodhisattva of Great Action,
to whom we bow in gratitude.
[BELL]

Listening deeply, serving beings in countless ways,
Avalokiteshvara, the Bodhisattva of Great Compassion,
to whom we bow in gratitude.
[BELL]

Fearless and persevering through realms of suffering and darkness,
Kshitigarbha, the Bodhisattva of Great Aspiration,
to whom we bow in gratitude.
[BELL]

Mother of buddhas, bodhisattvas, and all beings, nourishing,
holding, and healing all, Bodhisattva Gaia, Great Mother Earth,
precious jewel of the cosmos, to whom we bow in gratitude.
[BELL]

Radiating light in all directions, source of life on earth,
Mahavairocana Tathagata, Great Father Sun, Buddha of Infinite
Light and Life, to whom we bow in gratitude.
[BELL]

Showing the way fearlessly and compassionately,
the stream of all our ancestral teachers,
to whom we bow in gratitude.
[BELL]

4. OPENING VERSE ♪
[BELL, BELL, BELL]

Namo Tassa Bhagavato Arahato Samma Sambuddhassa
Namo Tassa Bhagavato Arahato Samma Sambuddhassa
Namo Tassa Bhagavato Arahato Samma Sambuddhassa
[BELL]

The Dharma is deep and lovely.
We now have a chance to see, study, and practice it.
We vow to realize its true meaning.
[BELL]

5. THE SUTRA OF THE INSIGHT THAT BRINGS US TO THE OTHER SHORE ♪

Avalokiteshvara, while practicing deeply
with the insight that brings us to the other shore,
suddenly discovered that all of the five skandhas are equally empty,
and with this realization he overcame all ill-being. [BELL]
"Listen Shariputra, this body itself is emptiness
and emptiness itself is this body.
This body is not other than emptiness
and emptiness is not other than this body.
The same is true of feelings, perceptions,
mental formations, and consciousness. [BELL]

"Listen Shariputra, all phenomena bear the mark of emptiness;
their true nature is the nature of no birth no death,

no being no nonbeing, no defilement no purity,
no increasing no decreasing. [BELL]

"That is why in emptiness, body, feelings,
perceptions, mental formations, and consciousness
are not separate self-entities.
The eighteen realms of phenomena, which are the six sense organs,
six sense objects, and six consciousnesses
are also not separate self-entities.
The Twelve Links of Interdependent Arising
and their extinction are also not separate self-entities.
Ill-being, the causes of ill-being,
the end of ill-being, the path, insight, and attainment,
are also not separate self-entities.
Whoever can see this
no longer needs anything to attain. [BELL]

"Bodhisattvas who practice the insight that brings us to the
other shore
see no more obstacles in their mind,
and because there are no more obstacles in their mind,
they can overcome all fear, destroy all wrong perceptions,
and realize perfect nirvana. [BELL]

"All buddhas in the past, present, and future
by practicing the insight that brings us to the other shore
are all capable of attaining authentic and perfect
enlightenment. [BELL]

"Therefore Shariputra, it should be known that
the insight that brings us to the other shore is a great mantra,
the most illuminating mantra, the highest mantra,
a mantra beyond compare,
the true wisdom that has the power
to put an end to all kinds of suffering. [BELL]

"Therefore let us proclaim a mantra
to praise the insight that brings us to the other shore
Gate gate paragate parasamgate bodhi svaha!

Gate gate paragate parasamgate bodhi svaha!
Gate gate paragate parasamgate bodhi svaha!"
[BELL BELL]

6. FORMAL REQUEST

[All aspirants requesting to receive Five Mindfulness Trainings are seated in the central aisle of the hall facing the altar, with their representative seated at the head of the group. The representative may be a lay member of the Order of Interbeing, or one of the aspirants.

The Aspirants' Representative
If there is anyone who has not had the time to apply to receive the transmission of the Five Mindfulness Trainings, but would like to receive them in today's ceremony, please stand up, announce your name and join the aspirants in the middle of the hall. [three breaths]

The Aspirants' Representative (with palms joined)
Namo Shakyamunaye Buddhaya.
Dear Respected Teacher, dear Noble Sangha, please listen to us with compassion. We would like to make a formal request.

[At the sound of the bell, the representative and all the aspirants touch the earth one time. They then kneel with palms joined.]

The Aspirants' Representative
Namo Shakyamunaye Buddhaya. Dear Respected Teacher, dear Noble Sangha, we recognize that we are very fortunate. Thanks to the many good seeds sown in us by our blood ancestors and spiritual ancestors, we have been lucky enough to discover the path of mindfulness. This path helps us to practice the art of stopping and living deeply in the present moment, so we can nourish, transform, and heal ourselves, and bring joy to ourselves and others. We know that the Five Mindfulness Trainings are a complete and beautiful expression of this path. Today, with all our heart, we aspire to receive the Five Precious Trainings from our spiritual ancestors and from you, the Noble Sangha. We understand clearly that following this path we will be in the company of bodhisattvas, and that every moment can be a moment of happiness. We humbly ask our dear spiritual ancestors and Noble Sangha to accept our request, and to transmit to us the Trainings.

The Transmission Master
We are happy to accept your request. You are very fortunate to have discovered this beautiful path and to have the opportunity to commit yourselves to it. In order to be able to continue on the path, you will always need a Sangha. It is very important for you to join or create a Sangha where you live, so you can realize your aspiration.

The Aspirants' Representative
We thank you dear Respected Teacher and dear Noble Sangha for accepting our request. We will follow your precious advice with all our heart.
[At the sound of the bell, the representative and all the aspirants touch the earth twice more. If the representative is not one of the aspirants, they then return to their place. All the aspirants remain in the center of the hall, and the ceremony begins.]

7. SANGHAKARMAN PROCEDURE

Sanghakarman Master: Has the entire community assembled?
Sangha Convener: The entire community has assembled.
Sanghakarman Master: Is there harmony in the community?
Sangha Convener: Yes, there is harmony.
Sanghakarman Master: Why has the community assembled today?
Sangha Convener: The community has assembled to perform the Sangha-karman of transmitting the Five Mindfulness Trainings.
Sanghakarman Master: Noble community, today, [date], has been chosen as the day to transmit the Five Mindfulness Trainings. The community has assembled at the appointed time and is ready to transmit and re-ceive the Five Mindfulness Trainings in an atmosphere of harmony. Thus, the transmission can proceed.
Is this statement clear and complete?
Everyone: Clear and complete.
[Repeat question and answer three times]
[BELL]

8. INTRODUCTORY WORDS

Today the community has gathered to give spiritual support to our broth-ers and sisters [names] who will make the vow to practice the Five Mind-

fulness Trainings. Will the entire community please enjoy your breathing and remain mindful when you hear the three sounds of the bell. The sound of the bell is the voice of the Buddha, bringing us back to our true home.
[BELL, BELL, BELL]

9. TOUCHING THE EARTH IN GRATITUDE

Ordinees, on hearing the sound of the bell, after the recitation of each line, please touch the earth one time.
In gratitude to our parents who have given us life,
we touch the earth before the Three Jewels.
[BELL]

In gratitude to our teachers who show us how to love,
understand, and live in the present moment,
we touch the earth before the Three Jewels.
[BELL]

In gratitude to our friends who guide us on the path
and support us in difficult moments,
we touch the earth before the Three Jewels.
[BELL]

In gratitude to all species in the animal, plant, and mineral worlds,
who support our life and make our world beautiful,
we touch the earth before the Three Jewels.
[BELL, BELL]

10. TRANSMITTING THE FIVE MINDFULNESS TRAININGS

Transmission Master
Dear friends, now is the time to transmit the Five Mindfulness Trainings. The Five Mindfulness Trainings represent the Buddhist vision for a global spirituality and ethic. They are a concrete expression of the Buddha's teachings on the Four Noble Truths and the Noble Eightfold Path, the path of right understanding and true love, leading to healing, transformation, and happiness for ourselves and for the world. To practice the Five Mindfulness Trainings is to cultivate the insight of interbeing, or Right View, which can remove all discrimination, intolerance, anger, fear, and despair.

If we live according to the Five Mindfulness Trainings, we are already on the path of a bodhisattva. Knowing we are on that path, we are not lost in confusion about our life in the present or in fears about the future.

We will now recite the Five Mindfulness Trainings. Listen carefully with a calm and clear mind. Say, *"Yes, I do"* every time you see you have the capacity to receive, learn, and practice the Mindfulness Trainings read. Dear friends, are you ready?
Ordinees: Yes, I am ready.

The First Mindfulness Training: Reverence for Life

Aware of the suffering caused by the destruction of life, I am committed to cultivating the insight of interbeing and compassion and learning ways to protect the lives of people, animals, plants, and minerals. I am determined not to kill, not to let others kill, and not to support any act of killing in the world, in my thinking, or in my way of life. Seeing that harmful actions arise from anger, fear, greed, and intolerance, which in turn come from dualistic and discriminative thinking, I will cultivate openness, nondiscrimination, and nonattachment to views in order to transform violence, fanaticism, and dogmatism in myself and in the world.

Transmission Master
This is the first of the Five Mindfulness Trainings. Do you make the commitment to receive, study, and practice it?
Ordinees: Yes, I do.
[BELL]
[*Ordinees touch the earth one time*]

The Second Mindfulness Training: True Happiness

Aware of the suffering caused by exploitation, social injustice, stealing, and oppression, I am committed to practicing generosity in my thinking, speaking, and acting. I am determined not to steal and not to possess anything that should belong to others; and I will share my time, energy, and material resources with those who are in need. I will practice looking deeply to see that the happiness and suffering of others are not separate from my own happiness and suffering; that true happiness is not possible without understanding and compassion; and that running after wealth, fame, power, and sensual pleasures can bring much suffering and despair.

I am aware that happiness depends on my mental attitude and not on external conditions, and that I can live happily in the present moment simply by remembering that I already have more than enough conditions to be happy. I am committed to practicing Right Livelihood so that I can help reduce the suffering of living beings on earth and reverse the process of global warming.

Transmission Master
This is the second of the Five Mindfulness Trainings. Do you make the commitment to receive, study, and practice it?
Ordinees: Yes, I do.
[BELL]
[*Ordinees touch the earth one time*]

The Third Mindfulness Training: True Love
Aware of the suffering caused by sexual misconduct, I am committed to cultivating responsibility and learning ways to protect the safety and integrity of individuals, couples, families, and society. Knowing that sexual desire is not love, and that sexual activity motivated by craving always harms myself as well as others, I am determined not to engage in sexual relations without mutual consent, true love, and a deep, long-term commitment. I resolve to find spiritual support for the integrity of my relationship from family members, friends, and sangha with whom there is support and trust. I will do everything in my power to protect children from sexual abuse and to prevent couples and families from being broken by sexual misconduct. Seeing that body and mind are interrelated, I am committed to learn appropriate ways to take care of my sexual energy and to cultivate the four basic elements of true love – loving kindness, compassion, joy, and inclusiveness – for the greater happiness of myself and others. Recognizing the diversity of human experience, I am committed not to discriminate against any form of gender identity or sexual orientation. Practicing true love, we know that we will continue beautifully into the future.

Transmission Master
This is the third of the Five Mindfulness Trainings. Do you make the commitment to receive, study, and practice it?
Ordinees: Yes, I do.
[BELL]
[*Ordinees touch the earth one time*]

The Fourth Mindfulness Training: Loving Speech and Deep Listening

Aware of the suffering caused by unmindful speech and the inability to listen to others, I am committed to cultivating loving speech and compassionate listening in order to relieve suffering and promote reconciliation and peace in myself and among other people, ethnic and religious groups, and nations. Knowing that words can create happiness or suffering, I am committed to speaking truthfully using words that inspire confidence, joy, and hope. When anger is manifesting in me, I am determined not to speak. I will practice mindful breathing and walking in order to recognize and look deeply into my anger. I know that the roots of anger can be found in my wrong perceptions and lack of understanding of the suffering in myself and in the other person. I will speak and listen in a way that can help myself and the other person to transform suffering and see the way out of difficult situations. I am determined not to spread news that I do not know to be certain and not to utter words that can cause division or discord. I will practice Right Diligence to nourish my capacity for understanding, love, joy, and inclusiveness, and gradually transform anger, violence, and fear that lie deep in my consciousness.

Transmission Master

This is the fourth of the Five Mindfulness Trainings. Do you make the commitment to receive, study, and practice it?
Ordinees: Yes, I do.
[BELL]
[Ordinees touch the earth one time]

The Fifth Mindfulness Training: Nourishment and Healing

Aware of the suffering caused by unmindful consumption, I am committed to cultivating good health, both physical and mental, for myself, my family, and my society by practicing mindful eating, drinking, and consuming. I will practice looking deeply into how I consume the Four Kinds of Nutriments, namely edible foods, sense impressions, volition, and consciousness. I am determined not to gamble, or to use alcohol, drugs, or any other products which contain toxins, such as certain websites, electronic games, TV programs, films, magazines, books, and conversations. I will practice coming back to the present moment to be in touch with the refreshing, healing, and nourishing elements in me and around me, not letting regrets and sorrow drag me back into the past nor letting anxieties, fear, or craving pull me out of the present moment. I am determined not to try to cover up loneliness, anxiety, or other suffering by losing myself in consumption. I will contemplate interbeing and consume in a way that preserves peace, joy, and well-being in my body and consciousness, and in the collective body and consciousness of my family, my society, and the earth.

Transmission Master
This is the fifth of the Five Mindfulness Trainings. Do you make the commitment to receive, study, and practice it?
Ordinees: Yes, I do.
[BELL]
[*Ordinees touch the earth one time*]

11. CONCLUDING WORDS

Dear friends, you have received the Five Mindfulness Trainings which are the foundation of happiness in the family and in society. They are the basis for the aspiration to help others. You should recite the trainings often, at least once a month, so that your understanding and practice of the Five Mindfulness Trainings can grow deeper every day.

A mindfulness trainings recitation ceremony can be organized in a practice center, with your local Sangha, or at home with friends. If you do not recite the trainings at least once in three months, you lose the transmission and today's ceremony will be nullified. Dear friends, as students of the Awakened One, you should be energetic in practicing the way the Buddha has taught to create peace and happiness for yourselves and all species. Upon hearing the sound of the bell, please stand up and bow deeply three times to show your gratitude to the Three Jewels.
[BELL, BELL, BELL]
[*Ordinees touch the earth three times*]

12. READING THE MINDFULNESS TRAININGS CERTIFICATE

Brothers and sisters, I will now read one Mindfulness Trainings Certificate. [the transmitter of the mindfulness trainings reads one certificate on which is written the Dharma lineage name of the ordinee and the name of the teacher.]

13. Closing the Ceremony

Noble community, to lend spiritual support to our brothers and sisters
who have been ordained, let us recite the closing verse in mindfulness:

Sharing the Merit ♪

Reciting the trainings, practicing the way of awareness
gives rise to benefits without limit.
We vow to share the fruits with all beings.
We vow to offer tribute to parents, teachers, friends,
and numerous beings
who give guidance and support along the path.
[BELL, BELL, BELL]

Ceremony to Transmit the Fourteen Mindfulness Trainings ॐ

[The Fourteen Mindfulness Trainings can only be transmitted in the name of venerable Thich Nhat Hanh by four dharma teachers who have received the lamp in the Plum Village tradition; and can be offered only to those who have successfull ompleted a minimum one-year mentoring program and have been formally accepted as ordinees. All members of the sangha, whether of the core or extended community may attend the ceremony.]

1. SITTING MEDITATION [12 MINUTES]

[All aspirants requesting to receive Fourteen Mindfulness Trainings are seated in the central aisle of the hall facing the altar, with their representative seated at the head of the group. The representative may be a lay member of the Order of Interbeing, or one of the aspirants. The rest of the community is seated on either side, in rows, by age of ordination.]

2. INCENSE OFFERING ♪

[BELL, BELL, BELL]
In gratitude, we offer this incense
throughout space and time
to all buddhas and bodhisattvas.
May it be fragrant as earth herself,
reflecting careful efforts,
wholehearted awareness,
and the fruit of understanding
slowly ripening.
May we and all beings
be companions of buddhas and bodhisattvas.
May we awaken from forgetfulness
and realize our true home.
[BELL]

3. Touching the Earth ♪

Introductory Verse
The one who bows and the one who is bowed to
are both, by nature, empty.
Therefore the communication between them
is inexpressibly perfect.
Our practice center is the net of Indra
reflecting all buddhas everywhere.
And with my person in front of each buddha,
I go with my whole life for refuge.
[BELL]

Touching the Earth
[*Touch the earth one time at the sound of each bell.*]
Offering light in the ten directions,
the Buddha, the Dharma, and the Sangha,
to whom we bow in gratitude.
[BELL]

Teaching and living the way of awareness
in the very midst of suffering and confusion,
Shakyamuni Buddha, the Fully Enlightened One,
to whom we bow in gratitude.
[BELL]

Cutting through ignorance, awakening our hearts and our minds,
Manjushri, the Bodhisattva of Great Understanding,
to whom we bow in gratitude.
[BELL]

Working mindfully, working joyfully for the sake of all beings,
Samantabhadra, the Bodhisattva of Great Action,
to whom we bow in gratitude.
[BELL]

Listening deeply, serving beings in countless ways,
Avalokiteshvara, the Bodhisattva of Great Compassion,
to whom we bow in gratitude.
[BELL]

Fearless and persevering through realms of suffering and darkness,
Kshitigarbha, the Bodhisattva of Great Aspiration,
to whom we bow in gratitude.
[BELL]

Mother of buddhas, bodhisattvas, and all beings, nourishing,
holding, and healing all, Bodhisattva Gaia, Great Mother Earth,
precious jewel of the cosmos, to whom we bow in gratitude.
[BELL]

Radiating light in all directions, source of life on earth,
Mahavairocana Tathagata, Great Father Sun, Buddha of Infinite
Light and Life, to whom we bow in gratitude.
[BELL]

Showing the way fearlessly and compassionately,
the stream of all our ancestral teachers,
to whom we bow in gratitude. [BELL]

4. Opening Verse ♪

[BELL, BELL, BELL]
Namo Tassa Bhagavato Arahato Samma Sambuddhassa
Namo Tassa Bhagavato Arahato Samma Sambuddhassa
Namo Tassa Bhagavato Arahato Samma Sambuddhassa
[BELL]

The Dharma is deep and lovely.
We now have a chance to see, study, and practice it.
We vow to realize its true meaning.
[BELL]

5. The Sutra of the Insight that Brings Us to the Other Shore ♪

Avalokiteshvara, while practicing deeply
with the insight that brings us to the other shore,
suddenly discovered that all of the five skandhas are equally empty,
and with this realization he overcame all ill-being. [BELL]

"Listen Shariputra, this body itself is emptiness
and emptiness itself is this body.
This body is not other than emptiness
and emptiness is not other than this body.
The same is true of feelings, perceptions,
mental formations, and consciousness. [BELL]

"Listen Shariputra, all phenomena bear the mark of emptiness;
their true nature is the nature of no birth no death,
no being no nonbeing, no defilement no purity,
no increasing no decreasing. [BELL]

"That is why in emptiness, body, feelings,
perceptions, mental formations, and consciousness
are not separate self-entities.
The eighteen realms of phenomena, which are the six sense organs,
six sense objects, and six consciousnesses
are also not separate self-entities.
The Twelve Links of Interdependent Arising
and their extinction are also not separate self-entities.
Ill-being, the causes of ill-being,
the end of ill-being, the path, insight, and attainment,
are also not separate self-entities.
Whoever can see this
no longer needs anything to attain. [BELL]

"Bodhisattvas who practice the insight that brings us to the
other shore
see no more obstacles in their mind,
and because there are no more obstacles in their mind,
they can overcome all fear, destroy all wrong perceptions,
and realize perfect nirvana. [BELL]

"All buddhas in the past, present, and future
by practicing the insight that brings us to the other shore
are all capable of attaining authentic and perfect
enlightenment. [BELL]

"Therefore Shariputra, it should be known that

the insight that brings us to the other shore is a great mantra,
the most illuminating mantra, the highest mantra,
a mantra beyond compare,
the true wisdom that has the power
to put an end to all kinds of suffering. [BELL]

"Therefore let us proclaim a mantra
to praise the insight that brings us to the other shore
Gate gate paragate parasamgate bodhi svaha!
Gate gate paragate parasamgate bodhi svaha!
Gate gate paragate parasamgate bodhi svaha!"
[BELL, BELL]

6. FORMAL REQUEST

The aspirants' representative (with palms joined)
Namo Sakyamunaye Buddhaya. Dear Respected Teacher, dear Noble
Sangha, please listen to us with compassion. We would like to make a
formal request.
[At the sound of the bell, the representative and all the aspirants touch the earth
one time. They then kneel with palms joined.]

The aspirants' representative (makes the request in the name of all the
aspirants)
Namo Sakyamunaye Buddhaya. Dear Respected Teacher, dear Noble
sangha, we recognize that we are very fortunate people in the world. We
have received much merit from our blood ancestors and spiritual ancestors
and, thanks to this, we have had the chance to receive and practice the Five
Mindfulness Trainings. The path of practice of the Trainings has helped
our love and understanding to grow, bringing transformation, healing, and
joy to ourselves and those around us. We have understood how valuable it
is on this path to have a sangha. Without the sangha, how could we have
been able to continue this beautiful practice in our daily life? If we flow
with our sangha as a river, we know we can reach the ocean of liberation.
We would like to embrace the sangha's career as our own. In the past year,
we have come together once a month to study the Fourteen Mindfulness
Trainings. We have participated regularly in mindfulness days and retreats
organized by our local sangha or Plum Village. Today, with all our heart,
we aspire to receive the Fourteen Precious Trainings from the Community

of Interbeing. We understand clearly that following this path we are in the company of bodhisattvas, and that every moment can be a moment of happiness. We humbly ask our dear spiritual ancestors and Noble Sangha to accept our request, and to transmit to us the Trainings.

The Transmission Master replies
We are happy to accept your request. You are very fortunate to have discovered such a wonderful path and to have the opportunity to commit yourselves to it. Your most beautiful task is to build a sangha that can be a place of refuge for many people. This is what the Buddha did his whole life. Following this path you continue the Buddha's career. The Buddha and all the bodhisattvas will support you.

The aspirants' representative offers thanks
We thank you dear Respected Teacher and dear Noble Sangha for accepting our request. We will follow your precious advice with all our heart.

[At the sound of the bell, the representative and all the aspirants touch the earth twice more. If the representative is not one of the aspirants, they then return to their place. All the aspirants remain in the center of the hall, and the ceremony begins.]

7. SANGHAKARMAN PROCEDURE

Sanghakarman Master: Has the entire community assembled?
Sangha Convener: The entire community has assembled.
Sanghakarman Master: Is there harmony in the community?
Sangha Convener: Yes, there is harmony.
Sanghakarman Master: Why has the community assembled today?
Sangha Convener: The community has assembled to perform the Sang-hakarman of transmitting the Fourteen Mindfulness Trainings of the Order of Interbeing.
Sanghakarman Master: Noble community please listen. Today, [date], has been chosen as the day to transmit the Fourteen Mindfulness Trainings of the Order of Interbeing. The community has assembled at the appointed time and is ready to transmit and receive the Fourteen Mindfulness Trainings in an atmosphere of harmony. Thus, the transmission can proceed. This is the proposal. Is the proposal clear and complete?
Is this statement clear and complete?
Everyone: Clear and complete.

8. TOUCHING THE EARTH IN GRATITUDE

[On hearing the sound of the bell, after the recitation of each line, touch the earth one time.]
In gratitude to our father and mother, who have given us life,
we bow deeply before the Three Jewels in the ten directions.
[BELL]

In gratitude to our teachers, who have shown us how to understand, love, and live deeply the present moment, we bow deeply before the Three Jewels in the ten directions.
[BELL]

In gratitude to our friends, who guide us and support us in difficult moments, we bow deeply before the Three Jewels in the ten directions.
[BELL]

In gratitude to all beings in the animal, plant, and mineral worlds,
we bow deeply before the Three Jewels in the ten directions.
[BELL, BELL]

9. INTRODUCTORY WORDS

Today the community has gathered to give spiritual support to our brothers and sisters at the solemn moment when they will undertake to receive and observe the Fourteen Mindfulness Trainings of the Order of Interbeing and enter the core community of the Order of Interbeing.

Ordinees, please listen. Following in the steps of the bodhisattvas as your teachers and companions on the path, you have made the aspiration to receive and observe the mindfulness trainings of the Order of Interbeing. You have given rise to the seed of bodhicitta, the mind of love. You have made it your aspiration to develop this seed. Your own awakening and liberation, as well as the liberation and awakening of all other species, have now become your highest career. Brothers and sisters in the community, please establish your mindfulness by enjoying your breathing, so that you may be truly present and give support to the seed of bodhicitta, the mind of love in the ordinees. With your support, they will develop this seed solidly and courageously so that it will become indestructible.

Ordinees, this is the solemn moment for receiving the Fourteen Mind-

fulness Trainings of the Order of Interbeing. Listen carefully, with a clear and concentrated mind, to each mindfulness training as it is read, and answer, "Yes, I do," clearly every time you see that you have the intention and capacity to receive, study, and practice the mindfulness training that has been read.
[BELL]

Brothers and sisters, are you ready?
Ordinees: Yes, I am ready.
These then are the Fourteen Mindfulness Trainings of the Order of Interbeing.

10. TRANSMITTING THE FOURTEEN MINDFULNESS TRAININGS

The First Mindfulness Training: Openness

Aware of the suffering created by fanaticism and intolerance, we are determined not to be idolatrous about or bound to any doctrine, theory, or ideology, even Buddhist ones. We are committed to seeing the Buddhist teachings as a guiding means that help us learn to look deeply and develop understanding and compassion. They are not doctrines to fight, kill, or die for. We understand that fanaticism in its many forms is the result is the result of perceiving things in a dualistic or discriminative manner. We will train ourselves to look at everything with openness and the insight of interbeing in order to transform dogmatism and violence in ourselves and the world.

This is the First Mindfulness Training of the Order of Interbeing. Do you make the commitment to receive, study, and practice it?
Ordinees: Yes, I do.
[BELL] *
[Ordinees touch the earth one time]

The Second Mindfulness Training: Nonattachment to Views

Aware of the suffering created by attachment to views and wrong perceptions, we are determined to avoid being narrow-minded and bound to

---

*When the bell master wishes the reader to proceed with the next training, they stop the sound of the bell by placing the inviter against the rim.

present views. We are committed to learning and practicing non-attach-
ment from views and being open to others' insights and experiences in
order to benefit from the collective wisdom. Insight is revealed through the
practice of compassionate listening, deep looking, and letting go of notions
rather than through the accumulation of intellectual knowledge. We are
aware that the knowledge we presently possess is not changeless, absolute
truth. Truth is found in life, and we will observe life within and around us
in every moment, ready to learn throughout our lives.

This is the Second Mindfulness Training of the Order of Interbeing. Do you
make the commitment to receive, study, and practice it?
Ordinees: Yes, I do.
[BELL]
[*Ordinees touch the earth one time*]

The Third Mindfulness Training: Freedom of Thought
Aware of the suffering brought about when we impose our view on others,
we are determined not to force others, even our children, by any means
whatsoever—such as authority, threat, money, propaganda, or indoctrination—to adopt our views. We are committed to respecting the rights of
others to be different, to choose what to believe and how to decide. We will,
however, learn to help others let go of and transform narrowness through
loving speech and compassionate dialogue.

This is the Third Mindfulness Training of the Order of Interbeing. Do you
make the commitment to receive, study, and practice it?
Ordinees: Yes, I do.
[BELL]
[*Ordinees touch the earth one time*]

The Fourth Mindfulness Training: Awareness of Suffering
Aware that looking deeply at the nature of suffering can help us cultivate understanding and compassion, we are determined to come home to
ourselves, to recognize, accept, embrace, and listen to our own suffering
with the energy of mindfulness. We will do our best not to run away from
our suffering or cover it up through consumption but practice conscious
breathing and walking to look deeply into the roots of our suffering. We
know we can only find the path leading to the transformation of suffering when we understand the roots of suffering. Once we have understood

our own suffering, we will be able to understand the suffering of others. We are committed to finding ways, including personal contact and using the telephone, electronic, audiovisual, and other means to be with those who suffer, so we can help them transform their suffering into compassion, peace and joy.

This is the Fourth Mindfulness Training of the Order of Interbeing. Do you make the commitment to receive, study, and practice it?
Ordinees: Yes, I do.
[BELL]
[Ordinees touch the earth one time]

The Fifth Mindfulness Training: Compassionate, Healthy Living
Aware that happiness is rooted in peace, solidity, freedom, and compassion, we are determined not to accumulate wealth while millions are hungry and dying nor to take as the aim of our life fame, profit, wealth, or sensual pleasure, which can bring much suffering and despair. We will practice looking deeply into how we nourish our body and mind with edible foods, sense impressions, volition, and consciousness. We are committed not to gamble or to use alcohol, drugs or any other products that bring toxins into our own and the collective body and consciousness such as certain websites, electronic games, tv programs, films, magazines, books, and conversations. We will consume in a way that preserves compassion, peace, joy, and well-being in our bodies and consciousness and in the collective body and consciousness of our families, our society, and the earth.

This is the Fifth Mindfulness Training of the Order of Interbeing. Do you make the commitment to receive, study, and practice it?
Ordinees: Yes, I do.
[BELL]
[Ordinees touch the earth one time]

The Sixth Mindfulness Training: Taking Care of Anger
Aware that anger blocks communication and creates suffering; we are committed to taking care of our energy of anger when it arises, to recognizing and transforming the seeds of anger that lie deep in our consciousness. When anger manifests, we are determined not to do or say anything, but to practice mindful breathing or mindful walking to acknowledge, embrace, and look deeply into our anger. We know that the roots of anger are not

outside of ourselves but can be found in our wrong perceptions and lack of understanding of the suffering in ourselves and the other person. By contemplating impermanence, we will be able to look with the eyes of compassion at ourselves and those we think are the cause of our anger, and to recognize the preciousness of our relationships. We will practice Right Diligence in order to nourish our capacity of understanding, love, joy and inclusiveness, gradually transforming our anger, violence, and fear and helping others do the same.

This is the Sixth Mindfulness Training of the Order of Interbeing. Do you make the commitment to receive, study, and practice it?
Ordinees: Yes, I do.
[BELL]
[*Ordinees touch the earth one time*]

The Seventh Mindfulness Training:
Dwelling Happily in the Present Moment
Aware that life is available only in the present moment, we are committed to training ourselves to live deeply each moment of daily life. We will try not to lose ourselves in dispersion or be carried away by regrets about the past, worries about the future, or cravings, anger, or jealousy in the present. We will practice mindful breathing to be aware of what is happening in the here and now. We are determined to learn the art of mindful living by touching the wondrous, refreshing, and healing elements that are inside and around us, in all situations. In this way, we will be able to cultivate seeds of joy, peace, love, and understanding in ourselves, thus facilitating the work of transformation and healing in our consciousness. We are aware that happiness depends primarily on our mental attitude and not on external conditions, and that we can live happily in the present moment simply by remembering that we already have more than enough conditions to be happy.

This is the Seventh Mindfulness Training of the Order of Interbeing. Do you make the commitment to receive, study, and practice it?
Ordinees: Yes, I do.
[BELL]
[*Ordinees touch the earth one time*]

The Eighth Mindfulness Training: True Community and Communication
Aware that lack of communication always brings separation and suffering, we are committed to training ourselves in the practice of compassionate listening and loving speech. Knowing that true community is rooted in inclusiveness and in the concrete practice of harmony of views, thinking, and speech, we will practice to share our understanding and experiences with members in our community in order to arrive at collective insight. We are determined to learn to listen deeply without judging or reacting, and refrain from uttering words that can create discord or cause the community to break. Whenever difficulties arise, we will remain in our Sangha and practice looking deeply into ourselves and others to recognize all the causes and conditions, including our own habit energies, that have brought about the difficulties. We will take responsibility for all the ways we may have contributed to the conflict and keep communication open. We will not behave as a victim but be active in finding ways to reconcile and resolve all conflicts however small.

This is the Eighth Mindfulness Training of the Order of Interbeing. Do you make the commitment to receive, study, and practice it?
Ordinees: Yes, I do.
[BELL]
[*Ordinees touch the earth one time*]

The Ninth Mindfulness Training: Truthful and Loving Speech
Aware that words can create happiness or suffering, we are committed to learning to speak truthfully, lovingly, and constructively. We will only use words that inspire joy, confidence, and hope as well as promote reconciliation and peace in ourselves and among people. We will speak and listen in a way that can help ourselves and others to transform suffering and see the way out of difficult situations. We are determined not to say untruthful things for the sake of personal interest or to impress people, nor to utter words that might cause division or hatred. We will protect the joy and harmony of our sangha by refraining from speaking about the faults of another person in their absence and always ask ourselves whether our perceptions are correct. We will speak only with the intention to understand and help transform the situation. We will not spread rumors nor criticize or condemn things of which we are not sure. We will do our best to speak out about situations of injustice, even when doing so may make difficulties for us or threaten our safety.

This is the Ninth Mindfulness Training of the Order of Interbeing. Do you make the commitment to receive, study, and practice it?
Ordinees: Yes, I do.
[BELL]
[*Ordinees touch the earth one time*]

The Tenth Mindfulness Training: Protecting and Nourishing the Sangha

Aware that the essence and aim of a sangha is the practice of understanding and compassion, we are determined not to use the Buddhist community for personal power or profit or transform our community into a political instrument. However, as members of a spiritual community, we should take a clear stand against oppression and injustice. We should strive to change the situation, without taking sides in a conflict. We are committed to looking with the eyes of interbeing and learning to see ourselves and others as cells in one sangha body. As a true cell in the sangha body, generating mindfulness, concentration, and insight to nourish ourselves and the whole community, each of us is at the same time a cell in the Buddha body. We will actively build brotherhood and sisterhood, flow as a river, and practice to develop the three real powers—love, understanding, and cutting through afflictions—to realize collective awakening.

This is the Tenth Mindfulness Training of the Order of Interbeing. Do you make the commitment to receive, study, and practice it?
Ordinees: Yes, I do.
[BELL]
[*Ordinees touch the earth one time*]

The Eleventh Mindfulness Training: Right Livelihood

Aware that great violence and injustice have been done to our environment and society, we are committed not to live with a vocation that is harmful to humans or nature. We will do our best to select a livelihood that contributes to the well-being of all species on earth and helps realize our ideal of understanding and compassion. Aware of economic, political and social realities around the world, as well as our interrelationship with ecosystem, we are determined to behave responsibly as consumers and citizens. We will not invest in or purchase from companies that contribute to the depletion of natural resources, harm the earth; and deprive others of the chance to live.

This is the Eleventh Mindfulness Training of the Order of Interbeing. Do you make the commitment to receive, study, and practice it?
Ordinees: Yes, I do.
[BELL]
[Ordinees touch the earth one time]

The Twelfth Mindfulness Training: Reverence for Life

Aware that much suffering is caused by war and conflict, we are determined to cultivate nonviolence, compassion, and the insight of interbeing in our daily lives and promote peace education, mindful mediation, and reconciliation within families, communities, ethnic and religious groups, nations, and in the world. We are committed not to kill and not to let others kill. We will not support any act of killing in the world, in our thinking or in our way of life. We will diligently practice deep looking with our Sangha to discover better ways to protect life, prevent war, and build peace.

This is the Twelfth Mindfulness Training of the Order of Interbeing. Do you make the commitment to receive, study, and practice it?
Ordinees: Yes, I do.
[BELL]
[Ordinees touch the earth one time]

The Thirteenth Mindfulness Training: Generosity

Aware of the suffering caused by exploitation, social injustice, stealing, and oppression, we are committed to cultivating generosity in our way of thinking, speaking, and acting. We will learn better ways to work for the well-being of people, animals, plants, and minerals and will practice generosity by sharing our time, energy, and material resources with those who are in need. We are determined not to steal and not to possess anything that should belong to others. We will respect the property of others, but will try to prevent others from profiting from human suffering or the suffering of other beings.

This is the Thirteenth Mindfulness Training of the Order of Interbeing. Do you make the commitment to receive, study, and practice it?
Ordinees: Yes, I do.
[BELL]
[Ordinees touch the earth one time]

The Fourteenth Mindfulness Training: True Love
[*For lay members*]: Aware that sexual desire is not love and that sexual relations motivated by craving cannot dissipate the feeling of loneliness but
will create more suffering, frustration, and isolation, we are determined
not to engage in sexual relations without mutual understanding, love, and
a deep long-term commitment. We resolve to find spiritual support for the
integrity of our relationships from family members, friends, and sangha
with whom there is support and trust. We know that to preserve the happiness of ourselves and others, we must respect the rights and commitments
of ourselves and others. Recognizing the diversity of human experience,
we are committed not to discriminate against any form of gender identity
or sexual orientation. Seeing that body and mind are interrelated, we are
committed to learning appropriate ways to take care of our sexual energy
and cultivating loving kindness, compassion, joy, and inclusiveness for our
own happiness and the happiness of others. We must be aware of future
suffering that may be caused by sexual relations. We will treat our bodies
with compassion and respect. We are determined to look deeply into the
Four Nutriments and learn ways to preserve and channel our vital energies
(sexual, breath, spirit) for the realization of our bodhisattva ideal. We will
do everything in our power to protect children from sexual abuse and to
protect couples and families from being broken by sexual misconduct.
We will be fully aware of the responsibility of bringing new lives into the
world, and will meditate regularly upon their future environment.

[*For monastic members*]: Aware that the deep aspiration of a monk or a nun
can only be realized when he or she wholly leaves behind the bonds of
sensual love, we are committed to practicing chastity and to helping others
protect themselves. We are aware that loneliness and suffering cannot be alleviated through a sexual relationship, but through practicing loving kindness, compassion, joy, and inclusiveness. We know that a sexual relationship
will destroy monastic life, will prevent us from realizing our ideal of serving
living beings, and will harm others. We will learn appropriate ways to take
care of sexual energy. We are determined not to suppress or mistreat our
body or to look upon our body as only an instrument, but to learn to handle
our body with compassion and respect. We are determined to look deeply
into the Four Nutriments in order to preserve and channel our vital energies
(sexual, breath, spirit) for the realization of our bodhisattva ideal.

This is the Fourteenth Mindfulness Training of the Order of Interbeing. Do
you make the commitment to receive, study, and practice it?

Ordinees: Yes, I do.
[BELL]
[*Ordinees touch the earth one time*]

11. CONCLUDING WORDS

Brothers and sisters, you have received the Fourteen Mindfulness Trainings of the Order of Interbeing. You have taken the first step on the path
of the bodhisattvas: the path of great understanding of bodhisattva Manjushri that puts an end to countless wrong perceptions, prejudice and discrimination; the path of great compassion of Bodhisattva Avalokitesvara,
who loves, values, and protects the life of all species and listens deeply to
the cries of all species far and near in order to help them; the path of great
action of bodhisattva Samantabhadra, who takes every opportunity to create love, understanding and harmony in the world.

Brothers and sisters in the community, with one heart please give your
spiritual support to the ordinees in this present moment to help them now
and in the future. Brothers and sisters, the buddhas and bodhisattvas will
be with you on your path of practice. When you hear the sound of the bell,
please stand up and bow deeply three times to show your gratitude to the
Three Jewels.

12. TRANSMISSION OF CERTIFICATE OF ORDINATION AND BROWN JACKET
[*if available*]

13. CLOSING THE CEREMONY

Noble community, to lend spiritual support to our brothers and sisters
who have been ordained, please recite the closing verses in mindfulness:

SHARING THE MERIT ♪

Transmitting. the trainings, practicing the way of awareness
gives rise to benefits without limit.
We vow to share the fruits with all beings.
We vow to offer tribute to parents, teachers, friends, and numerous beings
who give guidance and support along the path.
[BELL, BELL, BELL]

Beginning Anew Ceremony ॐ*

1. SITTING MEDITATION [12 MINUTES]

2. INCENSE OFFERING ♪

[BELL, BELL, BELL]
In gratitude, we offer this incense
throughout space and time
to all buddhas and bodhisattvas.
May it be fragrant as earth herself,
reflecting careful efforts,
wholehearted awareness,
and the fruit of understanding
slowly ripening.
May we and all beings
be companions of buddhas and bodhisattvas.
May we awaken from forgetfulness
and realize our true home.
[BELL]

3. TOUCHING THE EARTH ♪

Introductory Verse
The one who bows and the one who is bowed to
are both, by nature, empty.
Therefore the communication between them
is inexpressibly perfect.
Our practice center is the net of Indra
reflecting all buddhas everywhere.
And with my person in front of each buddha,
I go with my whole life for refuge.
[BELL]

---

*For more on the Beginning Anew practice, see Thich Nhat Hanh, *Teachings on Love* (Berkeley, CA: Parallax Press, 1997), and Thich Nhat Hanh, *Touching Peace* (Berkeley, CA: Parallax Press, 1992), pp. 55–57

Touching the Earth
[*Touch the earth one time at the sound of each bell.*]

Offering light in the ten directions,
the Buddha, the Dharma, and the Sangha,
to whom we bow in gratitude.
[BELL]

Teaching and living the way of awareness
in the very midst of suffering and confusion,
Shakyamuni Buddha, the Fully Enlightened One,
to whom we bow in gratitude.
[BELL]

Cutting through ignorance, awakening our hearts and our minds,
Manjushri, the Bodhisattva of Great Understanding,
to whom we bow in gratitude.
[BELL]

Working mindfully, working joyfully for the sake of all beings,
Samantabhadra, the Bodhisattva of Great Action,
to whom we bow in gratitude.
[BELL]

Listening deeply, serving beings in countless ways,
Avalokiteshvara, the Bodhisattva of Great Compassion,
to whom we bow in gratitude.
[BELL]

Fearless and persevering through realms of suffering and darkness,
Kshitigarbha, the Bodhisattva of Great Aspiration,
to whom we bow in gratitude.
[BELL]

Mother of buddhas, bodhisattvas, and all beings, nourishing,
holding, and healing all, Bodhisattva Gaia, Great Mother Earth,
precious jewel of the cosmos, to whom we bow in gratitude.
[BELL]

Radiating light in all directions, source of life on earth,
Mahavairocana Tathagata, Great Father Sun, Buddha of Infinite
Light and Life, to whom we bow in gratitude.
[BELL]

Showing the way fearlessly and compassionately,
the stream of all our ancestral teachers,
to whom we bow in gratitude.
[BELL, BELL]

4. Opening Verse ♪

[BELL, BELL, BELL]
Namo Tassa Bhagavato Arahato Samma Sambuddhassa
Namo Tassa Bhagavato Arahato Samma Sambuddhassa
Namo Tassa Bhagavato Arahato Samma Sambuddhassa
[BELL]

The Dharma is deep and lovely.
We now have a chance to see, study, and practice it.
We vow to realize its true meaning.
[BELL]

5. Beginning Anew Chant

I, your disciple
with my heart at peace and pure,
join my palms as a lotus bud
and turn respectfully to you
the great hero of loving kindness,
and conqueror of afflictions, Shakyamuni Buddha,
as I offer words of fervent repentance. [BELL]

I was not fortunate enough
to bring the teachings into my life earlier
and so lived in forgetfulness for a long time.
Obscured by ignorance, I have brought about suffering
and have made many foolish mistakes.
I and my ancestors

have sown our heart's garden with unwholesome seeds.
We have been responsible for killing, stealing,
sexual misconduct, and wrong speech.
Much of what we have said and done
has continued to do damage day after day.
I repent of these countless afflictions
that have obstructed my happiness.
I vow to begin anew from today. [BELL]

I see I have been thoughtless
and wandered from the path of mindfulness.
Ignorance and afflictions have accumulated in me
and created feelings of hatred and grief.
My mind is sometimes weary of life
and troubled by anxiety.
Because I have not understood others
I have been angry and resentful,
arguing and blaming,
courting suffering everyday,
making greater the rift between us.
There are days when we do not want
to speak to or look at each other,
and the internal knots last a long time.
Now I turn to the Three Jewels.
In sincere repentance I bow my head. [BELL]

I know that in my consciousness
are buried countless wholesome seeds of love and understanding,
and of peace and joy.
But because I have not known how to water them
the wholesome seeds have not sprouted fresh and green.
Overwhelmed by suffering
I have made my life dark.
I have grown used to chasing a distant happiness.
My mind is constantly occupied by the past
or travelling far into the future.
I am caught in a cycle of anger.
Unable to appreciate the precious things I have,
I trample on real happiness,

so suffering is there month after month, year after year.
Now before the altar, fragrant with incense
I vow to change and begin anew. [BELL]

With sincerity and respect,
I turn to the buddhas in the ten directions
and the bodhisattvas, the hearer disciples,
self-awakened buddhas, and the holy ones.
With deep regret I repent my repeated mistakes.
May the nectar of purity
extinguish the flames of my afflictions.
May the boat of the true Dharma
carry me out of resentment.
I vow to live in an awakened way,
to train according to the true teachings that have been transmitted.
I vow to practice mindful breathing and smiling
and diligently live in mindfulness. [BELL]

I vow to come back to myself
and live in the wonderful present moment,
to sow wholesome seeds in my heart's garden,
cultivating understanding and love.
I vow to learn to look deeply
and practice deep understanding,
to see the true nature of all that is
and free myself from the suffering
brought about by the notion of birth and death.
I vow to practice loving speech,
to love and care for others throughout the day,
bringing the source of joy to many places,
helping people to suffer less,
and repaying the deep gratitude I owe
to parents, teachers, and friends.
With faith I light up the incense of my heart.
I turn to the Compassionate One
and ask for protection on the wonderful path of practice.
I vow to train myself diligently
so that the fruits of the path can ripen.
[BELL, BELL]
[*Some moments of silence to see clearly our apsiration to begin anew*]

6. REPENTANCE GATHA

I have made many mistakes,
in my thinking, speaking, and bodily actions.
They come from craving, anger, and ignorance.
Now I bow my head and repent.
Buddha, please be my witness,
from now on I shall do differently.
I shall live my days in mindfulness
and not repeat the mistakes I have made in the past.
Homage to the bodhisattva who repents.
Homage to the bodhisattva who repents.
Homage to the bodhisattva who repents.

All wrongdoing arises from the mind.
When the mind is purified, what trace of wrong is left?
After repentance, my heart is light like the white clouds
that have always floated over the ancient forest in freedom.
[BELL, BELL]

7. THE FOUR RECOLLECTIONS ♪

The Blessèd One is worthy and fully self-awakened.
I bow before the Buddha.
[BELL]

The teaching is well expounded by the Blessèd One.
I pay homage to the Dharma.
[BELL]

The community of the Blessèd One's disciples has practiced well.
I pay respect to the Sangha.
[BELL]

The Noble Teacher in whom I take refuge
is the one who embodies and reveals the ultimate reality,
is the one who is worthy of all respect and offering,
is the one who is endowed with perfected wisdom,

is the one who is endowed with right understanding and compassionate action,
is the one who happily crossed to the shore of freedom,
is the one who looked deeply to know the world well,
is the highest charioteer, training humankind,
teaching gods and humans,
the Awakened One, the World-Honored One.
[BELL]

The Teaching given by my Noble Teacher
is the path I undertake, the teaching well-proclaimed,
is the teaching that can be realized right here and right now,
is the teaching that is immediately useful and effective,
is the teaching inviting all to come and see directly,
is the teaching that is leading to the good, the true, the beautiful,
extinguishing the fire of afflictions;
it is a teaching for all sensible people to realize for themselves.
[BELL]

Practicing the teachings, the noble community in which I take refuge
is the community that goes in the direction of goodness,
in the direction of truth,
in the direction of beauty,
in the direction of righteousness;
is the community that is composed of four pairs and eight kinds of holy people;
is the community that is worthy of offerings, worthy of great respect,
worthy of admiration, worthy of salutation;
is the community standing upon the highest fields of merit in all of the world.
[BELL]

The Mindfulness Trainings, the wholesome way of living taught by my Noble Teacher,
is the wonderful practice that remains unbroken,
that remains harmonious, that remains flawless, that remains refined;
is the wonderful practice that has the capacity to prevent wrongdoing and to prevent danger;

is the wonderful practice that has the capacity to protect self and others
and to reveal beauty;
is the wonderful practice that is leading to concentration, leading to
peacefulness, leading to insight, leading to non-fear;
is the wonderful practice that shows us the way to total emancipation
and long-lasting happiness.
[BELL]

8. MAY THE DAY BE WELL ♪

May the day be well and the night be well.
May the midday hour bring happiness too.
In every minute and every second,
may the day and night be well.
By the blessing of the Triple Gem,
may all things be protected and safe.
May all beings born in each of the four ways
live in a land of purity.
May all in the three realms be born upon lotus thrones.
May countless wandering souls
realize the three virtuous positions of the bodhisattva path.
May all living beings, with grace and ease,
fulfill the bodhisattva stages.

The countenance of the World-Honored One, like the full moon
or like the orb of the sun, shines with the light of clarity.
A halo of wisdom spreads in every direction,
enveloping all with love and compassion,
joy and equanimity.
Namo Shakyamunaye Buddhaya
Namo Shakyamunaye Buddhaya
Namo Shakyamunaye Buddhaya
[BELL]

9. TOUCHING THE EARTH IN REPENTANCE (OPTIONAL)
[*All touch the earth one time at the sound of each bell*]

The Buddha Vipashyin, to whom we bow in gratitude.
[BELL]
The Buddha Shikhin, to whom we bow in gratitude.
[BELL]
The Buddha Vishvabhu, to whom we bow in gratitude.
[BELL]
The Buddha Krakucchandha, to whom we bow in gratitude.
[BELL]
The Budha Konagamana, to whom we bow in gratitude.
[BELL]
The Buddha Kashyapa, to whom we bow in gratitude.
[BELL]
The Buddha Shakyamuni, to whom we bow in gratitude.
[BELL]
The Bodhisattva of Great Understanding, Manjushri,
to whom we bow in gratitude.
[BELL]
The Bodhisattva of Great Action, Samantabhadra,
to whom we bow in gratitude.
[BELL]
The Bodhisattva of Great Compassion, Avalokiteshvara,
to whom we bow in gratitude.
[BELL]
The Bodhisattva of the Great Vow, Kshitigarbha,
to whom we bow in gratitude.
[BELL]
The Venerable Kashyapa, to whom we bow in gratitude.
[BELL]
The Venerable Shariputra, to whom we bow in gratitude.
[BELL]
The Venerable Maudgalyayana, to whom we bow in gratitude.
[BELL]
The Venerable Upali, to whom we bow in gratitude.
[BELL]
The Venerable Ananda, to whom we bow in gratitude.
[BELL]

The Venerable Mahaprajapati, to whom we bow in gratitude.
[BELL, BELL]

10. PROTECTING AND TRANSFORMING

We, your disciples, who from beginningless time
have created so many obstacles out of ignorance,
being born and dying with no direction,
have now found confidence in the highest awakening.
However much we may have drifted on the ocean of suffering,
today we see clearly that there is a beautiful path.
We turn toward the light of loving kindness to direct us.
We bow deeply to the Awakened One and to our spiritual ancestors
who light up the path before us, guiding every step.
[BELL]

The wrongdoings and sufferings in our life
are brought about by craving, hatred, ignorance, and pride.
Today we begin anew to purify and free our hearts.
With awakened wisdom, bright as the sun and the full moon,
and immeasurable compassion to help beings
we resolve to live a wholesome life.
With all our heart, we go for refuge to the Three Jewels.
With the boat of loving kindness,
we cross over the ocean of suffering.
With the torch of insight, we leave behind the forest of confusion.
With determination, we learn, reflect, and practice.
Right View is the ground of our actions of body, speech, and mind.
We walk, stand, lie down, and sit in mindfulness.
Upright and dignified, we speak, smile, come in, and go out.

Whenever anger or anxiety enters our heart,
we are determined to breathe mindfully and come back to ourselves.
With every step, we walk in the Pure Land.
With every look, we see the Dharmakaya.
Diligent and attentive,
we guard our six senses as they touch sense objects.
We transform old habit energies

so that the heart's garden of awakening
blooms with hundreds of flowers.
We bring peace and joy to every household,
and plant wholesome seeds on countless paths.
We aspire to remain with the Sangha,
in order to help beings everywhere in the world.

May mountains and rivers be our witness in this moment
as we bow our heads
and request the Lord of Compassion
to embrace us.
[BELL, BELL]

11. THE THREE REFUGES ♪

I take refuge in the Buddha,
the one who shows me the way in this life.
I take refuge in the Dharma,
the way of understanding and of love.
I take refuge in the Sangha,
the community that lives in harmony and awareness.
[BELL]

Dwelling in the refuge of Buddha,
I clearly see the path of light and beauty in the world.
Dwelling in the refuge of Dharma,
I learn to open many doors on the path of transformation.
Dwelling in the refuge of Sangha,
shining light that supports me, keeping my practice free of obstruction.
[BELL]

Taking refuge in the Buddha in myself,
I aspire to help all people recognize their own awakened nature,
realizing the mind of love.
Taking refuge in the Dharma in myself,
I aspire to help all people fully master the ways of practice
and walk together on the path of liberation.
Taking refuge in the Sangha in myself,

I aspire to help all people build fourfold communities,
to embrace all beings and support their transformation.
[BELL, BELL]

12. Sharing the Merit ♪

Reciting the trainings, practicing the way of awareness
gives rise to benefits without limit.
We vow to share the fruits with all beings.
We vow to offer tribute to parents, teachers, friends,
and numerous beings
who give guidance and support along the path.
[BELL, BELL, BELL]

Vesak Ceremony, Bathing the Buddha ॐ

[The Buddha's birthday is celebrated in April-May. The decorations for this ceremony can be done by children and adults together.

In the Vietnamese tradition a small roof supported by and made of bamboo or wood and decorated with leaves and flowers is made for the statue of the baby buddha. the statue is set on a stone in the middle of a large basin of water. The statue can be a small doll with one hand pointing to the sky and the other hand pointing to the earth. in the early morning children go to find the flowers to decorate the roof. the water in the basin that is used to bathe the buddha is fragrant with flowers and herbs. at the edge of the water is a ladle (preferably of wood or coconut shell) to pour water over the statue during the ceremony. all the participants come up in turn to offer a flower to the buddha before bathing the statue.]

1. WALKING MEDITATION [30 MINUTES] OPTIONAL

2. SITTING MEDITATION [12 MINUTES]

3. INCENSE OFFERING ♪

[BELL, BELL, BELL]
In gratitude, we offer this incense
throughout space and time
to all buddhas and bodhisattvas.
May it be fragrant as earth herself,
reflecting careful efforts,
wholehearted awareness,
and the fruit of understanding
slowly ripening.
May we and all beings
be companions of buddhas and bodhisattvas.
May we awaken from forgetfulness
and realize our true home.
[BELL]

4. Touching the Earth ♪

Introductory Verse
The one who bows and the one who is bowed to
are both, by nature, empty.
Therefore the communication between them
is inexpressibly perfect.
Our practice center is the net of Indra
reflecting all buddhas everywhere.
And with my person in front of each buddha,
I go with my whole life for refuge.
[BELL]

Touching the Earth
[*Touch the earth one time at the sound of each bell.*]
Offering light in the ten directions,
the Buddha, the Dharma, and the Sangha,
to whom we bow in gratitude.
[BELL]

Teaching and living the way of awareness
in the very midst of suffering and confusion,
Shakyamuni Buddha, the Fully Enlightened One,
to whom we bow in gratitude.
[BELL]

Showing the way fearlessly and compassionately,
the stream of all our ancestral teachers,
to whom we bow in gratitude.
[BELL, BELL]

5. Introductory Words

Today the community has gathered to celebrate the birth of the Buddha
and to bathe the baby Buddha. Dear friends, two thousand six hundred
years ago in the town of Kapilavastu, a Buddha known as Shakyamuni
was born as a human being on this beautiful planet earth. He was a human
being just as we are, but in him understanding and love were developed
to a very high degree, and he became a fully awakened being. He was a

beautiful and precious flower in the garden of humanity, an udumbara flower that blooms only once every three thousand years.

6. THE THREE REFUGES (SONG) ♪

I take refuge in the Buddha,
the one who shows me the way in this life.
Namo Buddhaya, Namo Buddhaya, Namo Buddhaya
I take refuge in the Dharma,
the way of understanding and love.
Namo Dharmaya, Namo Dharmaya, Namo Dharmaya.
I take refuge in the Sangha,
the community of mindful harmony.
Namo Sanghaya, Namo Sanghaya, Namo Sanghaya.
Namo Buddhaya, Namo Dharmaya, Namo Sanghaya.

7. DHARMA WORDS
[*Chanted or read by head of ceremony*]

The Buddha is a flower of humanity
who practiced the Way for countless lives.
He appeared on this earth as a prince who left his royal palace
to practice at the foot of the Bodhi tree.
He conquered illusion.
When the morning star arose,
he realized the great path of awakening
and turned the wheel of the Dharma.
[BELL]

All species together take refuge with one-pointed mind
to realize the path of no birth.
All species together take refuge with one-pointed mind
to vow to realize the path of no birth.
[BELL]

Namo Tassa Bhagavato Arahato Samma Sambuddhassa
[BELL, BELL]

8. PRAISING THE BUDDHA ♪

The Buddha is like the fresh, full moon
that soars across the immense sky.
When the river of mind is truly calm,
the deep waters perfectly mirror
the radiance of the moon.

The countenance of the World-Honored One,
like the full moon or the orb of the sun,
shines forth bright wisdom's halo
embracing all with love, compassion, joy, and inclusiveness.

May the way of the Buddha grow ever more bright
and all beings receive the Dharma rain.
May compassion cool the flames of the world,
and wisdom shine through the clouds of confusion
revealing to all the path.

May Mother Earth be protected and safe.
May the people in the world be equal and free.
May the winds and the rains be in harmony.
May the land be at peace in all directions
and the people embrace the path.

May the Sangha practice diligently,
showing love and concern for one and all,
just as for our very own family.
Transforming our hearts and minds
we aspire to follow all great beings.

With one heart we vow to practice
the way of all bodhisattvas,
of Samantabhadra and Avalokiteshvara,
the way of perfected wisdom. [BELL, BELL]

9. VERSE FOR BATHING THE BUDDHA

Today we bathe the Tathagata.
Deep wisdom and clarity bring great happiness.
May all living beings who are overwhelmed by suffering
see the Dharmakaya in this very world.

10. RECITATION ♪

[You can chant Namo Shakymunaye Buddhaya or sing The Three Refuges song while everyone comes forward to offer a flower and bathe the baby Buddha one by one.]

11. SHARING THE MERIT ♪

Reciting the sutras, practicing the way of awareness
gives rise to benefits without limit.
We vow to share the fruits with all beings.
We vow to offer tribute to parents, teachers, friends,
and numerous beings
who give guidance and support along the path.
[BELL, BELL, BELL]

Rose Ceremony

[This Ceremony was instituted by the venerable Thich Nhat Hanh after he had experienced the living presence of his mother some four years after she had died. Thay wrote the book "A Rose For Your Pocket" so that we can appreciate the presence of our mother.

This ceremony, based on that book, nourishes our understanding, love, and gratitude for our parents. The room where the ceremony is performed can be decorated with flowers and lamps. Red and white roses, and pins to attach them to the lapels of the participants, need to be prepared in advance. During the ceremony there is an opportunity for musical performances which can help create a mindful and peaceful atmosphere.]

1. SITTING MEDITATION [12 MINUTES]

2. INCENSE OFFERING ♪

[BELL, BELL, BELL]
In gratitude, we offer this incense
throughout space and time
to all buddhas and bodhisattvas.
May it be fragrant as earth herself,
reflecting careful efforts,
wholehearted awareness,
and the fruit of understanding
slowly ripening.
May we and all beings
be companions of buddhas and bodhisattvas.
May we awaken from forgetfulness
and realize our true home.
[BELL]

3. TOUCHING THE EARTH ♪

Introductory Verse
The one who bows and the one who is bowed to
are both, by nature, empty.
Therefore the communication between them
is inexpressibly perfect.
Our practice center is the net of Indra
reflecting all buddhas everywhere.
And with my person in front of each buddha,
I go with my whole life for refuge.
[BELL]

Touching the Earth
[*Touch the earth one time at the sound of each bell.*]
Offering light in the ten directions,
the Buddha, the Dharma, and the Sangha,
to whom we bow in gratitude.
[BELL]

Showing love for parents,
the elder Mahamaudgalyayana
to whom we bow in gratitude
[BELL]

Showing the way fearlessly and compassionately,
the stream of all our ancestral teachers
to whom we bow in gratitude
[BELL, BELL]

4. FIRST MUSICAL OFFERING

[*Song or piece of music that may be connected to our appreciation of our parents and can set an atmosphere of serenity for the ensuing ceremony*]

5. INTRODUCTORY WORDS

Today the community has gathered to celebrate the Rose Ceremony. Please listen with a serene mind. The work of a father is like a great mountain. The loyalty and love of a mother are like clear spring water. We come together today to remember our parents who have given us birth. You can keep your father and mother in mind before the Buddha, Dharma, and Sangha, and light up your awareness of love, gratitude, and happiness.

6. Reading of *A Rose for Your Pocket*

The thought "mother" cannot be separated from that of "love." Love is sweet, tender, and delicious. Without love, a child cannot flower, an adult cannot mature. Without love, we weaken and wither. The day my mother died, I made this entry in my journal: "The greatest misfortune of my life has come!" Even an old person, when they lose their mother, doesn't feel ready. They too have the impression that they are not yet ripe, that they are suddenly alone. They feel as abandoned and unhappy as a young orphan.

Writings extolling the virtues of motherhood have existed since the beginning of time throughout the world. When I was a child I heard a simple poem about losing your mother, and it is still very important for me. If your mother is still alive, you may feel tenderness for her each time you read this, fearing this distant yet inevitable event.

> That year, although I was still very young,
> my mother left me,
> and I realized that I was an orphan.
> Everyone around me was crying.
> I suffered in silence. . .
> Allowing the tears to flow,
> I felt my pain soften.
> Evening enveloped Mother's tomb.
> The pagoda bell rang sweetly.
> I realized that to lose your mother
> is to lose the whole universe.

We swim in a world of tender love for many years, and, without even knowing it, we are quite happy there. Only after it is too late do we become aware of it.

There are moments after a fever when you have a bitter, flat taste in your mouth, and nothing tastes good. Only when your mother comes and tucks you in, gently pulls the covers over your chin, puts her hand on your burning forehead—is it really a hand, or is it the silk of heaven?—and gently whispers, "My poor darling!" do you feel restored, surrounded with the sweetness of maternal love. Her love is so fragrant.

Father's work is enormous, as huge as a mountain. Mother's devotion is overflowing, like water from a mountain spring. Maternal love is our first taste of love, the origin of all feelings of love. Our mother is the teacher who first teaches us love, the most important subject in life. Without my mother I could never have known how to love. Thanks to her I can love my neighbors. Thanks to her I can love all living beings. Through her I acquired my first notions of understanding and compassion. Mother is the foundation of all love, and many religious traditions recognize this and pay deep honor to a maternal figure, the Virgin Mary, the goddess Kuan Yin. Hardly an infant has opened their mouth to cry without their mother already running to the cradle. Mother is a gentle and sweet spirit who makes unhappiness and worries disappear. When the word "mother" is uttered, already we feel our hearts overflowing with love. From love, the distance to belief and action is very short.

In the West, we celebrate Mother's Day in May. I am from the countryside of Vietnam, and I had never heard of this tradition. One day, I was visiting the Ginza district of Tokyo with the monk Thien An, and we were met outside a bookstore by several Japanese students who were friends of his. One discreetly asked him a question, and then took a white carnation from her bag and pinned it on my robe. I was surprised and a little embarrassed. I had no idea what this gesture meant, and I didn't dare ask. I tried to act natural, thinking this must be some local custom.

When they were finished talking (I don't speak Japanese), Thien An and I went into the bookstore, and he told me that today was what is called Mother's Day. In Japan, if your mother is still alive, you wear a red flower on your pocket or your lapel, proud that you still have your mother. If she is no longer alive, you wear a white flower. I looked at the white flower on my robe and suddenly I felt so unhappy. I was as much an orphan as any other unhappy orphan; we orphans could no longer proudly wear red flowers in our buttonholes. Those who wear white flowers suffer, and their thoughts cannot avoid returning to their mother. They cannot forget that she is no longer there. Those who wear red flowers are so happy, knowing their mother is still alive. They can try to please her before she is gone and it is too late. I find this a beautiful custom. I propose that we do the same thing in Vietnam, and in the West as well.

Mother is a boundless source of love, an inexhaustible treasure. But unfortunately, we sometimes forget. A mother is the most beautiful gift life offers us. Those of you who still have your mother near, please don't wait for her death to say, "My God, I have lived beside my mother all these years without ever looking closely at her. Just brief glances, a few words exchanged—asking for a little pocket money or one thing or another." You cuddle up to her to get warm, you sulk, you get angry with her. You only complicate her life, causing her to worry, undermining her health, making her go to sleep late and get up early. Many mothers die young because of their children. Throughout her life we expect her to cook, wash, and clean up after us, while we think only about our grades and our careers. Our mothers no longer have time to look deeply at us, and we are too busy to look closely at them. Only when she is no longer there do we realize that we have never been conscious of having a mother.

Without love, filial devotion is just artificial. When love is present, that is enough, and there is no need to talk of obligation. To love your mother is enough. It is not a duty, it is completely natural, like drinking when you are thirsty. Every child must have a mother, and it is totally natural to love her. The mother loves her child, and the child loves their mother. The child needs their mother, and the mother needs her child. If the mother doesn't need her child, nor the child their mother, then this is not a mother, and this is not a child. It is a misuse of the words "mother" and "child."

When I was young, one of my teachers asked me, "What do you have to do when you love your mother?" I told him, "I must obey her, help her, take care of her when she is old, and pray for her, keeping the ancestral altar when she has disappeared forever behind the mountain." Now I know that his question was superfluous. If you love your mother, you don't have to do anything. You love her; that is enough. To love your mother is not a question of morality or virtue.

Please do not think I have written this to give a lesson in morality. Loving your mother is to your own benefit. A mother is like a spring of pure water. If you do not know how to profit from this, it is unfortunate for you. I simply want to bring this to your attention, to help you avoid one day complaining that there is nothing left in life for you. If a gift such as the presence of your own mother doesn't satisfy you, even if you are president of a large corporation or king of the universe, you probably will not be satisfied.

I would like to tell a story. Please don't think that I am thoughtless. It could have been that my sister didn't marry, and I didn't become a monk. In any case, we both left our mother—one to lead a new life beside the man she loved, and the other to follow an ideal of life that he adored. The night my sister married, my mother worried about a thousand and one things, and didn't even seem sad. But when we sat down at the table for some light refreshments, while waiting for our in-laws to come for my sister, I saw that my mother hadn't eaten a bite. She said, "For eighteen years she has eaten with us and today is her last meal here before going to another family's home to take her meals." My sister cried, her head bowing barely above her plate, and she said, "Mama, I won't get married." But she married nonetheless. As for me, I left my mother to become a monk. To congratulate those who are firmly resolved to leave their family to become a monk, one says that they are following the way of understanding; but I am not proud of it. I love my mother, but I also have an ideal, and to serve it I had to leave her—so much the worse for me.

In life, it is often necessary to make difficult choices. We cannot catch two fish at the same time, one in each hand. It is difficult, because if we accept growing up, we must accept suffering. I don't regret leaving my mother to become a monk, but I am sorry I had to make such a choice. I didn't have the chance to profit fully from this precious treasure. Each night I pray for my mother, but it is no longer possible for me to savor her presence. Please don't think that I am suggesting that you not follow your career and remain home at your mother's side. I have already said I do not want to give advice or lessons in morality. I only want to remind you that a mother is tenderness, she is love; so you, my brothers and sisters, please do not forget her. Forgetting creates an immense loss, and I hope you do not, either through ignorance or through lack of attention, have to endure such a loss. I gladly put a red flower, a rose, on your lapel so that you will be happy. That is all.

If I were to have any advice, it would be this: Tonight, when you return from school or work, or the next time you visit your mother, go into her room calmly, silently, with a smile, and sit down beside her. Without saying anything, make her stop working, and look at her for a long time. Look at her well, in order to see her well, in order to realize she is there, alive, sitting beside you. Then take her hand and ask her this short question, "Mother, do you know something?" She will be a little surprised, and will ask you, smiling, "What, dear?" Continuing to look into her eyes with a serene smile, tell her, "Do you know that I love you?" Ask her without waiting for an answer. Even if you are thirty, forty years old, or older, ask her simply because you are the child of your mother. Your mother and you will both be happy, conscious of living in eternal love. And tomorrow when she leaves you, you will not have any regrets.

This is the refrain I give you to sing today. Brothers and sisters, please chant it, please sing it, so you will not live in indifference or forgetfulness. This red rose, I have already placed it on your lapel. Please be happy. [BELL]

7. SECOND MUSICAL OFFERING

[Instrumental piece without words to be offered to our spiritual and blood ancestors.]

8. A FATHER'S LOVE

[Personal statement on a father's love read by someone.]

9. A MOTHER'S LOVE

[Personal statement on a mother's love read by someone.]

10. THIRD MUSICAL OFFERING

[Young people are invited to sing about the love they have been shown by their parents, with or without musical accompaniment.]

11. PINNING THE ROSES

[Several young people, beautifully dressed, come forward and kneel before the altar with their palms joined, they touch the earth one time, and then kneel before the elders. The elders ask the young people what color roses they need. A red rose represents a parent still alive, and a white rose represents a parent who is deceased. Then the elders pin to each young person on their left lapel the two roses. When the young people have each received two roses, the head of ceremony invites the bell to sound, and the young people touch the earth three times to express gratitude to their father and mother. After touching the earth, the young people stand up and turn to face the community in order to pin roses on other community members. For example, if there are six young people, then six people come up at a time with their palms joined and kneel down for the young people to pin on the roses. They tell the young people what color roses they need. The young people select two roses from trays next to them and pin the roses on the left lapels of the community members.

When these six community members have received two roses, they stand up, *walk toward the altar, and touch the earth three times before the Three Jewels to express their gratitude to their parents, accompanied by sounds of the bell. then they return to their seats. While they are touchiung the earth, six more people from the community come up and kneel before the six young people to receive their roses. This continues until everyone has received two roses and had the opportunity to bow.]*

12. Hugging Meditation between Parents and Children, if desired.

New Year's Ceremony ॐ

[The occasion of the new year is a wonderful time to practice beginning anew within ourselves, with family and friends, and as a community. In Plum Village, the whole community gathers on New Year's Eve to enjoy a mindful meal, artistic performances, and the new year's ceremony. Before the ceremony itself, there is a walking meditation where people bring their new year's aspiration written on a piece of paper. At some point during the walk, there is a brazier lit for burning the aspiration. The sitting meditation period is timed to end as the first few seconds of the new year begin. Then, the first activity of the community for the new year is this ceremony to pay respect to our teachers and our ancestors. An offering of fruit, flowers, and tea can be placed on the ancestral altar.]

1. SITTING MEDITATION [30 MINUTES]

2. INCENSE OFFERING ♪

[BELL, BELL, BELL]
In gratitude, we offer this incense
throughout space and time
to all buddhas and bodhisattvas.
May it be fragrant as earth herself,
reflecting careful efforts,
wholehearted awareness,
and the fruit of understanding
slowly ripening.
May we and all beings
be companions of buddhas and bodhisattvas.
May we awaken from forgetfulness
and realize our true home.
[BELL]

3. TOUCHING THE EARTH ♪

Introductory Verse
The one who bows and the one who is bowed to
are both, by nature, empty.
Therefore the communication between them
is inexpressibly perfect.
Our practice center is the net of Indra
reflecting all buddhas everywhere.
And with my person in front of each buddha,
I go with my whole life for refuge.
[BELL]

Touching the Earth
[*Touch the earth one time at the sound of each bell.*]

Offering light in the ten directions,
the Buddha, the Dharma, and the Sangha,
to whom we bow in gratitude.
[BELL]

Seed of awakening and loving kindness in children and all beings,
Maitreya, the Buddha to be born,
to whom we bow in gratitude.
[BELL]

Showing the way fearlessly and compassionately,
the stream of all our ancestral teachers
to whom we bow in gratitude
[BELL, BELL]

4. ADDRESS TO OUR ANCESTORS AT THE NEW YEAR

[*At this time, the entire community turns toward the ancestral altar. One stick of
incense is lit and held by one sangha member who is accompanied by the reader of
this New Year address as the whole community kneels before the altar.*]

Dear ancestors, both spiritual and genetic,
Breathing in, we are aware of your presence in us. You have never left us,

and we always carry you into the future. We know that in the past we have made many mistakes. We have lived a life of separation, hatred, loneliness, suffering, and despair. We have allowed individualism to prevail, and it has caused us much hardship and done much damage. We have learned that fame, wealth, power, and sensual pleasures cannot bring us true happiness. We also know that only love and compassion can make our lives meaningful and that we can learn to live as a sangha—a community, giving our children and our grandchildren a chance for a healthy and positive future.

As we gather as brothers and sisters, we become aware of your continued presence inside and around us. We would like to make this promise to you, our spiritual and blood ancestors, our brothers and sisters in the human family, and all our children and their children who are already here within us: On the occasion of the New Year, we shall learn to live in harmony and peace, in the heart of our family and our community, just as bees in the same hive and cells in the same body. We promise that we shall remain open-hearted and capable of communicating with members of our family and community. We promise always to listen deeply and to use peaceful and loving speech. We shall learn to listen to you, our ancestors, to understand your suffering and your hopes. We shall also listen to our brothers, sisters, friends, and children so that we may live in peace and harmony with them. We promise to learn to see the happiness and well-being of the community as our own happiness and well-being.

We know that this is the only way to assure a future for our children, ourselves and for the entire earth with all its species. In this solemn moment of the new year, we promise to you and to our children: We shall learn to breathe mindfully, to use the eyes and ears of the sangha, to live simply and to love without discrimination. Please help us, protect us, and protect our children. We promise to practice for you and for them so that joy, peace, and harmony will become possible again on earth. Please accept our offerings of incense, flowers, fruit, tea, and our love and faithfulness.

[After the address has been read, the incense stick is offered on the altar and the text of the address that has been read is given to the bell master who burns it. Then the whole community touches the earth four times to strengthen the vow that has just been read in everyone's heart.]
[BELL]

5. SHARING THE MERIT ♪

Reciting the sutras, practicing the way of awareness
gives rise to benefits without limit.
We vow to share the fruits with all beings.
We vow to offer tribute to parents, teachers, friends,
and numerous beings
who give guidance and support along the path.
[BELL, BELL, BELL]

6. LOOKING WITH THE EYES OF COMPASSION

[Participants are invited to turn to each other and practice looking deeply at each other in order to express their gratitude and enter into the New Year with open hearts and harmony.]

Wedding Ceremony ॐ

1. Walking Meditation outside [30 minutes]

2. Sitting Meditation [12 minutes]

3. Incense Offering ♪

[BELL, BELL, BELL]
In gratitude, we offer this incense
throughout space and time
to all buddhas and bodhisattvas.
May it be fragrant as earth herself,
reflecting careful efforts,
wholehearted awareness,
and the fruit of understanding
slowly ripening.
May we and all beings
be companions of buddhas and bodhisattvas.
May we awaken from forgetfulness
and realize our true home.
[BELL]

4. Touching the Earth ♪

Introductory Verse
The one who bows and the one who is bowed to
are both, by nature, empty.
Therefore the communication between them
is inexpressibly perfect.
Our practice center is the net of Indra
reflecting all buddhas everywhere.
And with my person in front of each buddha,
I go with my whole life for refuge.
[BELL]

Touching the Earth
[*Touch the earth one time at the sound of each bell.*]
Offering light in the ten directions,
the Buddha, the Dharma, and the Sangha,
to whom we bow in gratitude.
[BELL]

Teaching and living the way of awareness
in the very midst of suffering and confusion,
Shakyamuni Buddha, the Fully Enlightened One,
to whom we bow in gratitude.
[BELL]

Cutting through ignorance, awakening our hearts and our minds,
Manjushri, the Bodhisattva of Great Understanding,
to whom we bow in gratitude.
[BELL]

Working mindfully, working joyfully for the sake of all beings,
Samantabhadra, the Bodhisattva of Great Action,
to whom we bow in gratitude.
[BELL]

Listening deeply, serving beings in countless ways,
Avalokiteshvara, the Bodhisattva of Great Compassion,
to whom we bow in gratitude.
[BELL]

Fearless and persevering through realms of suffering and darkness,
Kshitigarbha, the Bodhisattva of Great Aspiration,
to whom we bow in gratitude.
[BELL]

Mother of buddhas, bodhisattvas, and all beings, nourishing,
holding, and healing all, Bodhisattva Gaia, Great Mother Earth,
precious jewel of the cosmos, to whom we bow in gratitude.
[BELL]

Radiating light in all directions, source of life on earth,
Mahavairocana Tathagata, Great Father Sun, Buddha of Infinite
Light and Life, to whom we bow in gratitude.
[BELL]

Showing the way fearlessly and compassionately,
the stream of all our ancestral teachers,
to whom we bow in gratitude.
[BELL, BELL]

5. OPENING VERSE ♪
[BELL, BELL, BELL]

Namo Tassa Bhagavato Arahato Samma Sambuddhassa
Namo Tassa Bhagavato Arahato Samma Sambuddhassa
Namo Tassa Bhagavato Arahato Samma Sambuddhassa
[BELL]

The Dharma is deep and lovely.
We now have a chance to see, study, and practice it.
We vow to realize its true meaning.
[BELL]

6. THE SUTRA OF THE INSIGHT THAT BRINGS US TO THE OTHER SHORE ♪

Avalokiteshvara, while practicing deeply
with the insight that brings us to the other shore,
suddenly discovered that all of the five skandhas are equally empty,
and with this realization he overcame all ill-being. [BELL]
"Listen Shariputra, this body itself is emptiness
and emptiness itself is this body.
This body is not other than emptiness
and emptiness is not other than this body.
The same is true of feelings, perceptions,
mental formations, and consciousness. [BELL]

"Listen Shariputra, all phenomena bear the mark of emptiness;
their true nature is the nature of no birth no death,

no being no nonbeing, no defilement no purity,
no increasing no decreasing. [BELL]

"That is why in emptiness, body, feelings,
perceptions, mental formations, and consciousness
are not separate self-entities.
The eighteen realms of phenomena, which are the six sense organs,
six sense objects, and six consciousnesses
are also not separate self-entities.
The Twelve Links of Interdependent Arising
and their extinction are also not separate self-entities.
Ill-being, the causes of ill-being,
the end of ill-being, the path, insight, and attainment,
are also not separate self-entities.
Whoever can see this
no longer needs anything to attain. [BELL]

"Bodhisattvas who practice the insight that brings us to the
other shore
see no more obstacles in their mind,
and because there are no more obstacles in their mind,
they can overcome all fear, destroy all wrong perceptions,
and realize perfect nirvana. [BELL]

"All buddhas in the past, present, and future
by practicing the insight that brings us to the other shore
are all capable of attaining authentic and perfect
enlightenment. [BELL]

"Therefore Shariputra, it should be known that
the insight that brings us to the other shore is a great mantra,
the most illuminating mantra, the highest mantra,
a mantra beyond compare,
the true wisdom that has the power
to put an end to all kinds of suffering. [BELL]

"Therefore let us proclaim a mantra
to praise the insight that brings us to the other shore
Gate gate paragate parasamgate bodhi svaha!

Gate gate paragate parasamgate bodhi svaha!
Gate gate paragate parasamgate bodhi svaha!"
[BELL, BELL]

7. INTRODUCTORY WORDS

Today the community gathers to lend spiritual support to our brother
[name] and our sister [name], in their taking the vow to practice the Five
Awarenesses. Please, everyone, follow your breathing in mindfulness
when you hear the three sounds of the bell.
[BELL, BELL, BELL]

Brother [name] and Sister [name], please come forward in front of the
altar, forming a lotus bud with your palms.

8. TOUCHING THE EARTH IN GRATITUDE

On hearing the sound of the bell, after the recitation of each line, please
touch the earth one time.
In gratitude to our father and mother, who have brought us to life, we bow
deeply before the Three Jewels in the ten directions.
[BELL]
In gratitude to our teachers, who have shown us the way to understand and
love, we bow deeply before the Three Jewels in the ten directions.
[BELL]
In gratitude to our friends, who guide and support us on our path, we bow
deeply before the Three Jewels in the ten directions.
[BELL]
In gratitude to all beings in the animal, plant, and mineral worlds, we bow
deeply before the Three Jewels in the ten directions.
[BELL, BELL]

9. THE FIVE AWARENESSES

Brother [name] and Sister [name], please kneel down.

Noble community, please listen. This is the moment when our brother
[name] and sister [name] will make the vow to practice the Five Awarenesses as they embark on their life as a couple. Students of the Buddha

are aware we inter-are and that happiness is not an individual matter. By living and practicing awareness, we bring peace and joy to our lives and the lives of those related to us. Brother and Sister, please repeat the Five Awarenesses after me, and say "Yes, I do" firmly if you intend to make the vow to practice them. After each Awareness, when you hear the sound of the bell, touch the earth before the Three Jewels.

The First Awareness
We are aware that all generations of our ancestors and all future generations are present in us.

This is the first of the Five Awarenesses. Do you make the vow to receive, study, and practice it?
Bride and groom together: "Yes, I do."
[BELL]
[*Bride and groom touch the earth one time*]

The Second Awareness
We are aware of the expectations that our ancestors, our children, and their children have of us.

This is the second of the Five Awarenesses. Do you make the vow to receive, study, and practice it?
Bride and groom together: Yes, I do.
[BELL]
[*Bride and groom touch the earth one time*]

The Third Awareness
We are aware that our joy, peace, freedom, and harmony are the joy, peace, freedom, and harmony of our ancestors, our children, and their children.

This is the third of the Five Awarenesses. Do you make the vow to receive, study, and practice it?
Bride and groom together: Yes, I do.
[BELL]
[*Bride and groom touch the earth one time*]

The Fourth Awareness
We are aware that understanding is the very foundation of love.

This is the fourth of the Five Awarenesses. Do you make the vow to receive, study, and practice it?
Bride and groom together: Yes, I do.
[BELL]
[*Bride and groom touch the earth one time*]

The Fifth Awareness
We are aware that blaming and arguing can never help us and only create a wider gap between us; that only understanding, trust, and love can help us change and grow.

This is the fifth of the Five Awarenesses. Do you make the vow to receive, study, and practice it?
Bride and groom together: Yes, I do.
[BELL, BELL]
[*Bride and groom touch the earth one time*]

10. STATEMENT OF SUPPORT

Brother [name] and Sister [name], you have made the solemn vow to study and practice the Five Awarenesses with the support of the Three Gems. As long as you continue to practice the Five Awarenesses, you continue to have the spiritual support of the Buddha, the Dharma, and the Sangha, and your happiness will be the happiness of many others. Each full-moon day, you should recite together these Five Awarenesses. This community wants to support you in this practice. Hearing the sound of the bell, please stand up and touch the earth three times before the Buddha, the Dharma, and the Sangha.
[*Bride and groom touch the earth three times*]

11. BOWING TO EACH OTHER

Brother and Sister, now is the time for you to face each other and bow deeply to each other to show your mutual respect. Your love and commitment will continue to grow based on this ground of mutual respect.
[*Bride and groom touch the earth one time*]

12. OFFERING OF RINGS [OPTIONAL] AND PROMISES*

Brother and Sister, please kneel down in front of each other. It is the time for you to exchange rings and promises.

13. INVOCATION OF THE BUDDHAS AND BODHISATTVAS ♪

Please, will the whole community invoke the names of the buddhas and the bodhisattvas in support of the newly-wedded couple.

[CHANT EACH NAME THREE TIMES]
Om Namo Shakyamunaye Buddhaya
[Homage to Shakyamuni Buddha, the Fully Awakened One]
[BELL]

Om Namo Manjushriye Bodhisattvaya
[Homage to Manjushri, Bodhisattva of Great Understanding]
[BELL]

Om Namo Samantabhadraya Bodhisattvaya [Homage to Samantabhadra, Bodhisattva of Great Action]
[BELL]

Om Namo Avalokiteshvaraya Bodhisattvaya
[Homage to Avalokiteshvara, Bodhisattva of Great Compassion]
[BELL]

Om Namo Kshitigarbhaya Bodhisattvaya
[Homage to Kshitigarbha, Bodhisattva of Great Aspiration]
[BELL, BELL]

14. THE THREE REFUGES ♪

I take refuge in the Buddha,
the one who shows me the way in this life.
I take refuge in the Dharma,
the way of understanding and of love.

* The promises are written by the bride and groom and read to each other.

I take refuge in the Sangha,
the community that lives in harmony and awareness.
[BELL]

Dwelling in the refuge of Buddha,
I clearly see the path of light and beauty in the world.
Dwelling in the refuge of Dharma,
I learn to open many doors on the path of transformation.
Dwelling in the refuge of Sangha,
shining light that supports me, keeping my practice free of obstruction.
[BELL]

Taking refuge in the Buddha in myself,
I aspire to help all people recognize their own awakened nature,
realizing the mind of love.
Taking refuge in the Dharma in myself,
I aspire to help all people fully master the ways of practice
and walk together on the path of liberation.
Taking refuge in the Sangha in myself,
I aspire to help all people build Fourfold Communities,
to embrace all beings and support their transformation.
[BELL, BELL]

15. SHARING THE MERIT ♪

Reciting the sutras, practicing the way of awareness
gives rise to benefits without limit.
We vow to share the fruits with all beings.
We vow to offer tribute to parents, teachers, friends,
and numerous beings
who give guidance and support along the path.
[BELL, BELL, BELL]

Offering Rice at Midday ૐ

---

1. INCENSE OFFERING ♪

As wonderful as the lotus flower,
as bright as the northern star,
let us come back and take refuge
in the teacher of gods and men.
[BELL]

In gratitude, we offer this incense
throughout space and time
to all buddhas and bodhisattvas.
May it be fragrant as earth herself,
reflecting careful efforts,
wholehearted awareness,
and the fruit of understanding
slowly ripening.
May we and all beings
be companions of buddhas and bodhisattvas.
May we awaken from forgetfulness
and realize our true home.
[BELL]

2. OFFERING CHANT

Homage to the Buddha abiding in the Ten Directions
Homage to the Dharma abiding in the Ten Directions
Homage to the Sangha abiding in the Ten Directions
Namo Shakyamunaye Buddhaya our Root Teacher
Namo Amitaya Buddhaya in the Land of Great Happiness
Homage to all Buddhas in the Ten Directions and the Three Times
Homage to the Bodhisattva of Great Understanding, Manjushri
Homage to the Bodhisattva of Great Action, Samantabhadra
Homage to the Bodhisattva of Great Compassion, Avalokiteshvara
Homage to the Bodhisattva of Great Strength, Mahasthamaprapta
Homage to the Bodhisattva of Great Aspiration, Kshitigarbha

Homage to the Bodhisattvas of the Holy Sangha present in this place of practice,
Homage to the Bodhisattvas our ancestral teachers of all generations,
Homage to the Bodhisattva who oversees the kitchen
Homage to the ten Bodhisattvas who are judges of the dead
Homage to all Buddhas and Bodhisattvas present in this practice center

3. Mantra Recitation

[Each mantra to be recited three times, or simply concentrate to visualize food being available to the hungry and water being available to the thirsty]

Mantra to Make Food Universally Available
Namah sarvatathagata'valokite.
Om sambhara sambhara hung.
[BELL]

Mantra to Make Water Universally Available
Namah surupaya tathagataya Tadyatha,
Om surupaya surupaya surupaya svaha.
[BELL, BELL]

4. Offering Gatha

The color, fragrance, and taste of this food
is offered first to all buddhas,
then to all the holy ones,
and to the people of the six continents.
The offering is made so that all, without distinction,
may have enough to eat.
May those who have given this food
cross over to the other shore.
Everything that is in the Dharma realms
is also offering the Three Qualities and the Six Flavors
to the Buddha and the Sangha.
[BELL]

5. GATHA

In concentration we make this offering of Dharma nectar
in quantity as great as Mount Sumeru.
Its form, fragrance, beauty, and taste fill the whole of space.
Please be compassionate to us and accept it.

Homage to the Bodhisattva of Universal Offering.
Homage to the Bodhisattva of Universal Offering.
Homage to the Bodhisattva of Universal Offering.
[BELL]

6. SHARING THE MERIT ♪

Making this offering, practicing the way of awareness
gives rise to benefits without limit.
We vow to share the fruits with all beings.
We vow to offer tribute to parents, teachers, friends,
and numerous beings who give guidance and support along the path.
[BELL]

With this offering to the Buddha
we vow that all beings
may fully realize
their career of great awakening.
[BELL, BELL, BELL]

Offering to the Hungry Ghosts ॐ

[The object of our offering in this ceremony is first and foremost the lonely soul. These are souls who do not have a place of refuge. Usually when someone dies there are those who will perform a funeral service for them. They have a family to do this and they have a place they call home. There are souls who have no ancestral home and there is no place for them in society. They feel very isolated. These are the hungry ghosts.

We offer food to hungry ghosts as a practice of compassion. We know that there are invisible beings or souls who suffer greatly and our offering is essentially one of understanding and love. The food is a representation of this offering.

An altar to the hungry ghosts is placed outside or near an open window, and on it are placed two candles, one stick of incense, rice gruel, uncooked rice grains, salt, and drinking water. Offerings of food suitable to each culture can be used, such as bread, fruit, soymilk, peanut butter, and so on.]

1. OPENING THE CEREMONY ♪

[Three sounds of the small bell are invited preceded by a crescendo of seven wake up sounds. The celebrant lights the incense stick and holds it high in mindfulness and concentration while three sounds of the large bell are invited. After that they place the stick in the incense holder.]

2. OPENING VERSE ♪

[BELL, BELL, BELL]
Namo Tassa Bhagavato Arahato Samma Sambuddhassa
Namo Tassa Bhagavato Arahato Samma Sambuddhassa
Namo Tassa Bhagavato Arahato Samma Sambuddhassa
[BELL]

The Dharma is deep and lovely.
We now have a chance to see, study, and practice it.
We vow to realize its true meaning.
[BELL]

3. DISCOURSE ON LOVE

"Those who want to attain peace should practice being upright, humble, and capable of using loving speech. They will know how to live simply and happily, with senses calmed, without being covetous and carried away by the emotions of the majority. Let them not do anything that will be disapproved of by the wise ones.

"(And this is what they contemplate:)

"May everyone be happy and safe, and may their hearts be filled with joy.

"May all beings live in security and in peace—beings who are frail or strong, tall or short, big or small, visible or not visible, near or far away, already born or yet to be born. May all of them dwell in perfect tranquility.

"Let no one do harm to anyone. Let no one put the life of anyone in danger. Let no one, out of anger or ill will, wish anyone any harm.

"Just as a mother loves and protects her only child at the risk of her own life, cultivate boundless love to offer to all living beings in the entire cosmos. Let our boundless love pervade the whole universe, above, below, and across. Our love will know no obstacles. Our heart will be absolutely free from hatred and enmity. Whether standing or walking, sitting or lying, as long as we are awake, we should maintain this mindfulness of love in our own heart. This is the noblest way of living.

"Free from wrong views, greed, and sensual desires, living in beauty and realizing Perfect Understanding, those who practice boundless love will certainly transcend birth and death."

4. THE SUTRA OF THE INSIGHT THAT BRINGS US TO THE OTHER SHORE ♪

Avalokiteshvara, while practicing deeply
with the insight that brings us to the other shore,
suddenly discovered that all of the five skandhas are equally empty,
and with this realization he overcame all ill-being. [BELL]
"Listen Shariputra, this body itself is emptiness
and emptiness itself is this body.
This body is not other than emptiness
and emptiness is not other than this body.
The same is true of feelings, perceptions,
mental formations, and consciousness. [BELL]

"Listen Shariputra, all phenomena bear the mark of emptiness;
their true nature is the nature of no birth no death,
no being no nonbeing, no defilement no purity,
no increasing no decreasing. [BELL]

"That is why in emptiness, body, feelings,
perceptions, mental formations, and consciousness
are not separate self-entities.
The eighteen realms of phenomena, which are the six sense organs,
six sense objects, and six consciousnesses
are also not separate self-entities.
The Twelve Links of Interdependent Arising
and their extinction are also not separate self-entities.
Ill-being, the causes of ill-being,
the end of ill-being, the path, insight, and attainment,
are also not separate self-entities.
Whoever can see this
no longer needs anything to attain. [BELL]

"Bodhisattvas who practice the insight that brings us to the other shore
see no more obstacles in their mind,
and because there are no more obstacles in their mind,
they can overcome all fear, destroy all wrong perceptions,
and realize perfect nirvana. [BELL]

"All buddhas in the past, present, and future
by practicing the insight that brings us to the other shore
are all capable of attaining authentic and perfect
enlightenment. [BELL]

"Therefore Shariputra, it should be known that
the insight that brings us to the other shore is a great mantra,
the most illuminating mantra, the highest mantra,
a mantra beyond compare,
the true wisdom that has the power
to put an end to all kinds of suffering. [BELL]

"Therefore let us proclaim a mantra
to praise the insight that brings us to the other shore

Gate gate paragate parasamgate bodhi svaha!
Gate gate paragate parasamgate bodhi svaha!
Gate gate paragate parasamgate bodhi svaha!"
[BELL BELL]

5. RECOLLECTION

Homage to Buddhas and Bodhisattvas in the Avatamsaka Assembly.
Homage to Buddhas and Bodhisattvas in the Avatamsaka Assembly.
Homage to Buddhas and Bodhisattvas in the Avatamsaka Assembly.

Homage to the Bodhisattva of the Hungry Ghost Realm.
Homage to the Bodhisattva of the Hungry Ghost Realm.
Homage to the Bodhisattva of the Hungry Ghost Realm.
[BELL, BELL]

6. INTRODUCTORY VERSE

As if a fire is raging on all four sides,
a hungry ghost ceaselessly suffers from heat.
Hungry ghosts, if you wish to be born in a pure land,
hear this verse transmitted by Buddha:

Those who aspire to see and understand
the buddhas who are present in the three times
should look deeply into the true nature of things
and see that all arises from the mind.
[BELL]

7. VISUALIZATIONS
VISUALIZATION FOR TRANSFORMING THE HELL REALMS

Let us be mindful of a situation of extreme suffering that may have happened in or near the place of this offering and see the situation being transformed. [BELL]

INVITATION TO THE HUNGRY GHOSTS
Let us be mindful of lonely souls coming to receive our offering of understanding and love. [BELL]

UNTYING THE KNOT OF INJUSTICE

Let us be mindful of those who have died in or near this place feeling much resentment at the injustice done to them and send them our compassion.
[BELL]

8. RECOLLECTION (EACH LINE IS REPEATED THREE TIMES)

Homage to the Avatamsaka Sutra proclaimed by the Buddhas in all directions.
[BELL]
Homage to the Buddhas present in the ten directions.
[BELL]
Homage to the Dharma present in the ten directions.
[BELL]
Homage to the Sangha present in the ten directions.
[BELL]
Homage to Shakyamuni Buddha
[BELL]
Homage to Bodhisattva Avalokiteshvara
[BELL]
Homage to Bodhisattva Kshitigarbha
[BELL]
Homage to Ananda who recorded the teachings.
[BELL, BELL]

9. REPENTANCE AND ASPIRATION

Practitioners of the Way have acted unskillfully
with craving, hatred, and ignorance
manifested in actions of body, speech, and mind.
All practitioners repent of this.
[BELL]

Beings of all species have acted unskillfully
with craving, hatred, and ignorance
manifested in actions of body, speech, and mind.
All beings repent of this.
[BELL]

Hungry ghosts have acted unskillfully
with craving, hatred, and ignorance
manifested in actions of body, speech, and mind.
All hungry ghosts repent of this.
[BELL]

I vow to save countless beings,
to put an end to infinite afflictions,
to practice limitless Dharma doors,
and realize the highest path of awakening.
[BELL]

I vow to save living beings according to the true nature,
to put an end to afflictions according to the true nature,
to practice Dharma doors according to the true nature,
and realize the path of awakening according to the true nature.

10. VISUALIZATIONS

PUTTING AN END TO THE OBSTACLES OF UNWHOLESOME KARMA
Let us be mindful of the unwholesome karma committed by those who
have died here and see it being transformed into wholesome action. [BELL]

OPENING THE THROAT OF THE HUNGRY GHOST
Let us be mindful of the hearts of lonely souls opening so that they
receive our compassion and understanding. [BELL]

SPRINKLING WATER ON THE HEAD OF THE HUNGRY GHOST
Let us visualize annointing the head of the lonely souls with water
consecrated by understanding and love. [BELL]

MULTIPLYING THE FOOD
Let us visualize the food on the offering table being multiplied by the
power of the Buddha for all those who are hungry. (The rice grains are
thrown into the air so that they fall on the earth). [BELL]

MULTIPLYING THE WATER
Let us visualize the water on the offering table being multiplied by the
power of the Buddha for all those who are thirsty. [BELL]

CONSECRATING WATER SO IT HAS THE EIGHT VIRTUES
Let us visualize water as clear, cool, sweet, light in texture, sparkling bright, calm, eliminating hunger and thirst, and nourishing the practice. (The water is thrown in the air so that it falls on the earth.) [BELL]

11. VERSES OF OFFERING

Homage to the Tathagata Many Jewels
Homage to the Tathagata Precious Victory
Homage to the Tathagata Wonderful Form Body
Homage to the Tathagata Extensive Body
Homage to the Tathagata Far from Fear
Homage to the Tathagata of the Nectar of Compassion
Homage to the Tathagata of Infinite Light and Life
[BELL]

Maintaining our concentration, we purify this food,
and offer it to practitioners in the ten directions.
May they all be satisfied, letting go of craving,
and soon leave behind darkness to be born in a pure land.
May they take refuge in the Three Jewels,
give rise to awakened mind, and realize the highest path,
May the merit of this practice be there in the future
and be received by all of you, practitioners.
[BELL]

Maintaining our concentration, we purify this food,
and offer it to all species in the ten directions.
May they all be satisfied, letting go of craving,
moving out of darkness to be born into a pure land.
May they take refuge in the Three Jewels,
give rise to awakened mind, and realize the highest path,
May the merit of this practice be there in the future
and be received by all the non-human species.
[BELL]

Maintaining our concentration, we purify this food,
and offer it to hungry ghosts in the ten directions.
May they all be satisfied, letting go of craving,

moving out of darkness to be born into a pure land.
May they take refuge in the Three Jewels,
give rise to awakened mind, and realize the highest path,
May the merit of this practice be there in the future
and be received by all hungry ghosts.
[BELL]

O practitioners of the Way,
we make offerings of food
multiplied in ten directions
so that you can all receive them.
By the merit of this offering,
may we and all practitioners
be successful in the realization of the path.
[BELL]

O beings of all species,
we make offerings of food
multiplied in ten directions
so that you can all receive them.
By the merit of this offering,
may we and all species
be successful in the realization of the path.
[BELL]

O hungry ghosts,
we make offerings of food
multiplied in ten directions
so that you can all receive them.
By the merit of this offering,
may we and all hungry ghosts
be successful in the realization of the path.
[BELL]

12. VISUALIZATIONS

Let us visualize the offering of food being received equally by all beings
everywhere. [BELL]

13. CONCLUDING THE OFFERING

We offer up this fragrant nectar
in quantity as vast as space.
May all species realize their aspiration,
to come back and take refuge in the embrace of great loving kindness.
[BELL]

14. THE THREE REFUGES ♪

I take refuge in the Buddha,
the one who shows me the way in this life.
I take refuge in the Dharma,
the way of understanding and of love.
I take refuge in the Sangha,
the community that lives in harmony and awareness.
[BELL]

Dwelling in the refuge of Buddha,
I clearly see the path of light and beauty in the world.
Dwelling in the refuge of Dharma,
I learn to open many doors on the path of transformation.
Dwelling in the refuge of Sangha,
shining light that supports me, keeping my practice free of obstruction.
[BELL]

Taking refuge in the Buddha in myself,
I aspire to help all people recognize their own awakened nature,
realizing the mind of love.
Taking refuge in the Dharma in myself,
I aspire to help all people fully master the ways of practice
and walk together on the path of liberation.
Taking refuge in the Sangha in myself,
I aspire to help all people build fourfold communities,
to embrace all beings and support their transformation.
[BELL, BELL]

15. SHARING THE MERIT ♪

Reciting the sutras, practicing the way of awareness
gives rise to benefits without limit.
We vow to share the fruits with all beings.
We vow to offer tribute to parents, teachers, friends,
and numerous beings
who give guidance and support along the path.
[BELL]

May all be born in the Pure Land.
As the lotus of liberation blooms,
may we realize the truth of no-birth and no-death.
May buddhas and bodhisattvas be our companions
on the path of practice.
[BELL]

May we end all afflictions
so that understanding can arise,
the obstacles of unwholesome acts be dissolved,
and the fruit of awakening be fully realized.
[BELL, BELL, BELL]

Ceremony to Support the Sick ꩜

[*This ceremony is to offer peace of mind and courage to the sick and to those who have been victims of disasters as well as to their relatives and friends.*]

1. OPENING THE CEREMONY
Sitting meditation (12 minutes)

INCENSE OFFERING ♪

[BELL, BELL, BELL]
In gratitude, we offer this incense
throughout space and time
to all buddhas and bodhisattvas.
May it be fragrant as earth herself,
reflecting careful efforts,
wholehearted awareness,
and the fruit of understanding
slowly ripening.
May we and all beings
be companions of buddhas and bodhisattvas.
May we awaken from forgetfulness
and realize our true home.
[BELL]

TOUCHING THE EARTH ♪

OPENING GATHA

The one who bows and the one who is bowed to
are both, by nature, empty.
Therefore the communication between them
is inexpressibly perfect.
Our practice center is the net of Indra
reflecting all buddhas everywhere.

And with my person in front of each buddha,
I go with my whole life for refuge.
[BELL]

TOUCHING THE EARTH

[TOUCH THE EARTH ONE TIME AT THE SOUND OF EACH BELL.]
Offering light in the ten directions,
the Buddha, the Dharma, and the Sangha,
to whom we bow in gratitude.
[BELL]

Teaching and living the way of awareness
in the very midst of suffering and confusion,
Shakyamuni Buddha, the Fully Enlightened One,
to whom we bow in gratitude.
[BELL]

Cutting through ignorance, awakening our hearts and our minds,
Manjushri, the Bodhisattva of Great Understanding,
to whom we bow in gratitude.
[BELL]

Working mindfully, working joyfully for the sake of all beings,
Samantabhadra, the Bodhisattva of Great Action,
to whom we bow in gratitude.
[BELL]

Listening deeply, serving beings in countless ways,
Avalokiteshvara, the Bodhisattva of Great Compassion,
to whom we bow in gratitude.
[BELL]

Fearless and persevering through realms of suffering and darkness,
Kshitigarbha, the Bodhisattva of Great Aspiration,
to whom we bow in gratitude.
[BELL]

Mother of buddhas, bodhisattvas, and all beings, nourishing,
holding, and healing all, Bodhisattva Gaia, Great Mother Earth,
precious jewel of the cosmos, to whom we bow in gratitude.
[BELL]

Radiating light in all directions, source of life on earth,
Mahavairocana Tathagata, Great Father Sun, Buddha of Infinite
Light and Life, to whom we bow in gratitude.
[BELL]

Showing the way fearlessly and compassionately,
the stream of all our ancestral teachers,
to whom we bow in gratitude.
[BELL, BELL]

2. OPENING VERSE ♪
[BELL, BELL, BELL]

Namo Tassa Bhagavato Arahato Samma Sambuddhassa
Namo Tassa Bhagavato Arahato Samma Sambuddhassa
Namo Tassa Bhagavato Arahato Samma Sambuddhassa
[BELL]

The Dharma is deep and lovely.
We now have a chance to see, study, and practice it.
We vow to realize its true meaning.
[BELL]

3. MINDFULNESS OF LOVED ONES
Brothers and sisters, it is time to bring our loved ones to mind: those to
whom we wish to send the healing energy of love and compassion. Let us
sit and enjoy our breathing for a few moments, allowing our beloved ones
to be present with us now.
[TEN BREATHS IN SILENCE]

4. THE LOTUS OF THE WONDERFUL DHARMA: UNIVERSAL DOOR CHAPTER

Brothers and sisters, please listen. The peace and joy of the entire world, including the worlds of the living and the dead, depend on our own peace and joy in this moment. With all our heart and one-pointed mind, let us chant the Lotus of the Wonderful Dharma.

Buddha of ten thousand beautiful aspects,
may I ask you this question:
"Why did they give this bodhisattva
the name Avalokita?"
The World-Honored One, wonderfully adorned,
offered this reply to Akṣayomati:
"Because actions founded on her deep aspiration
can respond to the needs of any being in any circumstance.

"Her aspirations as wide as the oceans
were made for countless lifetimes.
She has attended to limitless buddhas,
her great aspiration purified by mindfulness.

"When anyone hears her name or sees her image,
if they give rise to right mindfulness
they will be able to overcome
the suffering of all the worlds."

"When those with cruel intent
push us into a pit of fire,
as we invoke the strength of Avalokita,
the fire becomes a lotus lake.

"Adrift on the waters of the great ocean,
threatened by monsters of the deep,
as we invoke the strength of Avalokita,
we are saved from the storm waves.

"Standing atop Mount Meru,
if someone should push us down,

as we invoke the strength of Avalokita,
we dwell unharmed like the sun in space.

"Chased by a cruel person
down the diamond mountain,
as we invoke the strength of Avalokita,
not even an eyelash will be in danger.

"Encircled and assaulted by bandits
holding swords to wound and to kill,
as we invoke the strength of Avalokita,
the bandits feel our suffering.

"Persecuted by kings and ministers,
about to be executed,
as we invoke the strength of Avalokita,
sword blades shatter into pieces.

"Imprisoned or bound in iron chains,
with hands and feet placed in a yoke,
as we invoke the strength of Avalokita,
we are released into freedom.

"Poisons, curses, and bewitchings
putting us into danger,
as we invoke the strength of Avalokita,
harmful things return to their source.

"Attacked by a fierce and cruel yaksha,
a poisonous naga, or unkind spirit,
as we invoke the strength of Avalokita,
they will do us no harm.

"With wild animals all around
baring their teeth, tusks, and claws,
as we invoke the strength of Avalokita,
they run far away.

"Confronted with scorpions and poisonous snakes,
breathing fire and poisonous smoke,

as we invoke the strength of Avalokita,
they depart, the air clears.

"Caught beneath lightning, thunder, and clouds,
with hail pouring down in torrents,
as we invoke the strength of Avalokita,
the storm ends, the sunlight appears.

"All living beings caught in distress,
oppressed by immeasurable suffering
are rescued in ten thousand ways
by the wonderful power of her understanding.

"Miraculous power with no shortcoming,
wisdom and skillful means so vast —
in the ten directions of all the worlds,
there is no place she does not appear.

"The paths to realms of suffering,
the pain of birth, old age, sickness, and death,
hells, hungry spirits, or animals
are gradually purified.

"Look of truth, look of purity,
look of boundless understanding,
look of love, look of compassion —
the look to be always honored and practiced.

"Look of immaculate light and purity,
the Sun of Wisdom destroying darkness,
master of fire, wind, and disaster
illuminating the whole world.

"Heart of compassion like rolling thunder,
heart of love like gentle clouds,
water of Dharma nectar raining upon us,
extinguishing the fire of afflictions.

"In the courtroom, the place of lawsuits,
on the fields in the midst of war,

as we invoke the strength of Avalokita,
our enemies become our friends.

"Sound of wonder, sublime sound,
sound of one looking deeply into the world,
sound of the rising tide, the sound that surpasses worldly sounds,
the sound of which we should always be mindful.

"With mindfulness, free from doubts,
when facing catastrophe and death,
Avalokita is the pure and holy one
in whom we need to take refuge.

"We bow in gratitude to the one
who has all the virtues,
regarding the world with compassionate eyes,
an ocean of merit beyond measure."

5. INTRODUCTORY WORDS
[*Adapt as appropriate.*]

Today the community has gathered to recite the sutra, practice mindfulness of the Buddha, and give spiritual support and offer peace to [name]. There are relatives and friends of [name] present with us to join in giving spiritual support. Brothers and sisters, listen carefully. Once one person is able to give rise to a deep sense of peace and happiness, the whole world benefits. We have gathered today to light the lamp of peace and happiness in our hearts by practicing sitting meditation, walking meditation, reciting the Lotus Sutra, and being mindful of the Buddha in order to be in communion with the essence of great love, compassion, joy, equanimity, and fearlessness. These are motivating forces that can transform situations of fear and danger and restore peace and happiness where they have been lost. The peace and joy of the world depend on our peace and joy at this moment. With all our concentration and a one-pointed mind, let us recite the name of Avalokiteshvara:

Namo'valokiteshvaraya ♪
[*repeat nine times*]
[BELL, BELL]

6. PRAISING THE BODHISATTVA OF COMPASSION ♪

The nectar of compassion is seen on the willow branch
held by the Bodhisattva.
A single drop of this nectar is enough to bring life
to the ten directions of the cosmos.
May all afflictions of this world disappear totally and
may this place of practice be completely purified
by the Bodhisattva's nectar of compassion.

Homage to the Bodhisattva who refreshes the earth.

From the depths of understanding, a flower of great eloquence blooms:
The Bodhisattva stands majestically
upon the waves of birth and death, free from all afflictions.
Her great compassion eliminates all sickness,
even that once thought of as incurable.
Her wondrous light sweeps away all obstacles and dangers.
Her willow branch, once waved,
reveals countless buddha lands.
Her lotus flower blossoms a multitude of practice centers.
We bow to her. We see her true presence in the here and the now.
We offer her the incense of our hearts.
May the Bodhisattva of Deep Listening embrace us all
with great compassion.

Namo'valokiteshvaraya
[Homage to Bodhisattva Avalokiteshvara]
[BELL, BELL]

7. MAY THE DAY BE WELL ♪

May the day be well and the night be well.
May the midday hour bring happiness too.
In every minute and every second,
may the day and night be well.
By the blessing of the Triple Gem,
may all things be protected and safe.
May all beings born in each of the four ways

live in a land of purity.
May all in the Three Realms be born upon Lotus thrones.
May countless wandering souls
realize the three virtuous positions of the bodhisattva path.
May all living beings, with grace and ease,
fulfill the bodhisattva stages.
The countenance of the World-Honored One, like the full moon
or like the orb of the sun, shines with the light of clarity.
A halo of wisdom spreads in every direction,
enveloping all with love and compassion,
joy and equanimity.

Namo Shakyamunaye Buddhaya
Namo Shakyamunaye Buddhaya
Namo Shakyamunaye Buddhaya
[BELL, BELL]

8. PROTECTING AND TRANSFORMING

We, your disciples, who from beginningless time
have created so many obstacles out of ignorance,
being born and dying with no direction,
have now found confidence in the highest awakening.
However much we may have drifted on the ocean of suffering,
today we see clearly that there is a beautiful path.
We turn toward the light of loving kindness to direct us.
We bow deeply to the Awakened One and to our spiritual ancestors
who light up the path before us, guiding every step.
[BELL]

The wrongdoings and sufferings in our life
are brought about by craving, hatred, ignorance, and pride.
Today we begin anew to purify and free our hearts.
With awakened wisdom, bright as the sun and the full moon,
and immeasurable compassion to help beings
we resolve to live a wholesome life.
With all our heart, we go for refuge to the Three Jewels.
With the boat of loving kindness,
we cross over the ocean of suffering.

With the torch of insight, we leave behind the forest of confusion.
With determination, we learn, reflect, and practice.
Right View is the ground of our actions of body, speech, and mind.
We walk, stand, lie down, and sit in mindfulness.
Upright and dignified, we speak, smile, come in, and go out.

Whenever anger or anxiety enters our heart,
we are determined to breathe mindfully and come back to ourselves.
With every step, we walk in the Pure Land.
With every look, we see the Dharmakaya.
Diligent and attentive,
we guard our six senses as they touch sense objects.
We transform old habit energies
so that the heart's garden of awakening
blooms with hundreds of flowers.
We bring peace and joy to every household,
and plant wholesome seeds on countless paths.
We aspire to remain with the Sangha,
in order to help beings everywhere in the world.

May mountains and rivers be our witness in this moment
as we bow our heads
and request the Lord of Compassion
to embrace us.
[BELL, BELL]

9. THE THREE REFUGES ♪

I take refuge in the Buddha,
the one who shows me the way in this life.
I take refuge in the Dharma,
the way of understanding and of love.
I take refuge in the Sangha,
the community that lives in harmony and awareness.
[BELL]

Dwelling in the refuge of Buddha,
I clearly see the path of light and beauty in the world.

Dwelling in the refuge of Dharma,
I learn to open many doors on the path of transformation.
Dwelling in the refuge of Sangha,
shining light that supports me, keeping my practice free of obstruction.
[BELL]

Taking refuge in the Buddha in myself,
I aspire to help all people recognize their own awakened nature,
realizing the mind of love.
Taking refuge in the Dharma in myself,
I aspire to help all people fully master the ways of practice
and walk together on the path of liberation.
Taking refuge in the Sangha in myself,
I aspire to help all people build fourfold communities,
to embrace all beings and support their transformation.
[BELL, BELL]

10. SHARING THE MERIT ♪

Reciting the sutras, practicing the way of awareness
gives rise to benefits without limit.
We vow to share the fruits with all beings.
We vow to offer tribute to parents, teachers, friends,
and numerous beings
who give guidance and support along the path.
[BELL, BELL, BELL]

11. WORDS OF GRATITUDE

[At this time, a relative or friend of the sick person is invited to come mindfully
before the community to offer a few words of gratitude to everyone who
participated in the ceremony.]

Ceremony to Support the Dying ॐ

[This ceremony is to offer peace of mind and non-fear to one who is dying and their relatives and friends.]

1. OPENING THE CEREMONY

Sitting meditation (12 minutes)

INCENSE OFFERING ♪
[BELL, BELL, BELL]

In gratitude, we offer this incense
throughout space and time
to all buddhas and bodhisattvas.
May it be fragrant as earth herself,
reflecting careful efforts,
wholehearted awareness,
and the fruit of understanding
slowly ripening.
May we and all beings
be companions of buddhas and bodhisattvas.
May we awaken from forgetfulness
and realize our true home.
[BELL]

TOUCHING THE EARTH ♪

OPENING GATHA

The one who bows and the one who is bowed to
are both, by nature, empty.
Therefore the communication between them
is inexpressibly perfect.
Our practice center is the net of Indra

reflecting all buddhas everywhere.
And with my person in front of each buddha,
I go with my whole life for refuge.
[BELL]

TOUCHING THE EARTH
[Touch the earth one time at the sound of each bell.]

Offering light in the ten directions,
the Buddha, the Dharma, and the Sangha,
to whom we bow in gratitude.
[BELL]

Teaching and living the way of awareness
in the very midst of suffering and confusion,
Shakyamuni Buddha, the Fully Enlightened One,
to whom we bow in gratitude.
[BELL]

Cutting through ignorance, awakening our hearts and our minds,
Manjushri, the Bodhisattva of Great Understanding,
to whom we bow in gratitude.
[BELL]

Working mindfully, working joyfully for the sake of all beings,
Samantabhadra, the Bodhisattva of Great Action,
to whom we bow in gratitude.
[BELL]

Listening deeply, serving beings in countless ways,
Avalokiteshvara, the Bodhisattva of Great Compassion,
to whom we bow in gratitude.
[BELL]

Fearless and persevering through realms of suffering and darkness,
Kshitigarbha, the Bodhisattva of Great Aspiration,
to whom we bow in gratitude.
[BELL]

Mother of buddhas, bodhisattvas, and all beings, nourishing,
holding, and healing all, Bodhisattva Gaia, Great Mother Earth,
precious jewel of the cosmos, to whom we bow in gratitude.
[BELL]

Radiating light in all directions, source of life on earth,
Mahavairocana Tathagata, Great Father Sun, Buddha of Infinite
Light and Life, to whom we bow in gratitude.
[BELL]

Showing the way fearlessly and compassionately,
the stream of all our ancestral teachers,
to whom we bow in gratitude.
[BELL, BELL]

2. OPENING VERSE ♪
[BELL, BELL, BELL]

Namo Tassa Bhagavato Arahato Samma Sambuddhassa
Namo Tassa Bhagavato Arahato Samma Sambuddhassa
Namo Tassa Bhagavato Arahato Samma Sambuddhassa
[BELL]

The Dharma is deep and lovely.
We now have a chance to see, study, and practice it.
We vow to realize its true meaning.
[BELL]

3. DISCOURSE ON THE TEACHINGS TO BE GIVEN TO THE SICK

I heard these words of the Buddha one time when the Lord was staying in
the monastery in the Jeta Grove in Anathapindika's park, near Shravasti.
At that time the householder Anathapindika was seriously ill. When the
Venerable Shariputra was told this, he immediately went to Ananda and
said, "Brother Ananda, let us go and visit the layman Anathapindika.

The Venerable Ananda put on his robe, and holding his bowl, went into the
town of Shravasti with the Venerable Shariputra to make the almsround.

The two of them stopped at every house until they came to the house of the layman Anathapindika, and they went in to visit him. After he had sat down, the Venerable Shariputra asked the layman Anathapindika, "How is your illness? Is it getting better or worse? Is the physical pain easing at all or is it getting greater?" The householder Anathapindika replied, "Venerable monks, it does not seem to be getting better. The pain is not easing. It is getting greater all the time." Shariputra said, "Friend Anathapindika, let us now practice together the recollection of the Buddha, the Dharma, and the Sangha. The recollection goes like this:

"The Buddha has gone to suchness, is fully and truly awakened, has perfected understanding and action, has arrived at true happiness, understands the nature of the world, is unequaled in understanding, has conquered the afflictions of human beings, is a teacher of gods and humans, and is the Awakened One, the one who liberates the world.

"The Dharma is the teaching of love and understanding that the Tathagata has expounded. It is deep and lovely, worthy of the highest respect, and very precious. It is a teaching that cannot be compared to ordinary teachings. It is a path of practice for the noble ones.

"The Sangha is the community of practice, guided by the teachings of the Tathagata. The community is in harmony, and within it all aspects of the practice can be realized. The community is respected and precious. It practices the precepts and realizes concentration, insight, and liberation. The sangha is the highest field of merit in the world.

"Friend Anathapindika, if you recollect the Buddha, the Dharma, and the Sangha in this way, the beneficial effects are beyond measure. Recollecting in this way, you can put an end to the obstacles of wrong deeds and the afflictions. You can harvest a fruit that is as fresh and sweet as the nectar of deathlessness. Anyone practicing an upright way of life who knows how to recollect the Three Jewels will have no chance of falling into the three lower realms but will be reborn as a human or a god.

"Friend Anathapindika, now is the time to practice the meditation on the six sense bases:

"These eyes are not me. I am not caught in these eyes.

"These ears are not me. I am not caught in these ears.

"This nose is not me. I am not caught in this nose.

"This tongue is not me. I am not caught in this tongue.

"This body is not me. I am not caught in this body.

"This mind is not me. I am not caught in this mind.

"Now continue your meditation with the six sense objects:

"These forms are not me. I am not caught in these forms.

"These sounds are not me. I am not caught in these sounds.

"These smells are not me. I am not caught in these smells.

"These tastes are not me. I am not caught in these tastes.

"These contacts with the body are not me. I am not caught in these contacts with the body.

"These thoughts are not me. I am not caught in these thoughts.

"Now continue your meditation on the six sense consciousnesses:

"Sight is not me. I am not caught in sight.

"Hearing is not me. I am not caught in hearing.

"Smelling is not me. I am not caught in smelling.

"Tasting is not me. I am not caught in tasting.

"Somatosensory consciousness is not me. I am not caught in somatosensory consciousness.

"Mind consciousness is not me. I am not caught in mind consciousness.

"Now continue your meditation on the six elements:

"The earth element is not me. I am not caught in the earth element.

"The water element is not me. I am not caught in the water element.

"The fire element is not me. I am not caught in the fire element.

"The air element is not me. I am not caught in the air element.

"The space element is not me. I am not caught in the space element.

"The consciousness element is not me. I am not caught in the consciousness element.

"Now continue your meditation on the five aggregates:

"Form is not me. I am not limited by form.

"Feelings are not me. I am not limited by feelings.

"Perceptions are not me. I am not limited by perceptions.

"Mental formations are not me. I am not limited by mental formations.
"Consciousness is not me. I am not limited by consciousness.

"Now continue your meditation on the three times:

"The past is not me. I am not limited by the past.
"The present is not me. I am not limited by the present.
"The future is not me. I am not limited by the future.

"Friend Anathapindika, everything arises and ceases due to causes and conditions. In reality, the nature of everything is not born and does not die, does not come and does not go. When eyes arise, they arise, but they do not come from anywhere. When eyes cease to be, they cease to be, but they do not go anywhere. Eyes are neither nonexistent before they arise, nor are they existent after they arise. Everything that is comes to be because of a combination of causes and conditions. When the causes and conditions are sufficient, eyes are present. When the causes and conditions are not sufficient, eyes are absent. The same is true of ears, nose, tongue, body, and mind; form, sound, smell, taste, touch, and thought; sight, hearing, smelling, tasting, somatosensory and mind conscioussness; the Six Elements, the Five Aggregates, and the Three Times.

"In the Five Aggregates, there is nothing that we can call 'I,' a 'person,' or a 'lifespan.' Ignorance is the inability to see this truth. Because there is ignorance, there are wrong perceptions of formations. Because there are wrong perceptions of formations, there is wrong consciousness. Because there is wrong consciousness, there is the distinction between the perceiver and the perceived. Because there is the distinction between the perceiver and the perceived, there is the distinction between the six organs and the six objects of sense. Because there is the distinction between the six organs and the six objects of sense, there is contact. Because there is contact, there is feeling. Because there is feeling, there is craving. Because there is craving, there is grasping. Because there is grasping, there is being and then birth, death, and the inexpressible mass of suffering and grief.

"Friend Anathapindika, you have meditated that everything that arises is due to causes and conditions and does not have a separate self. That is called 'the meditation on emptiness.' It is the highest and the most profound meditation."

When he had practiced to this point, the layman Anathapindika began to cry and tears flowed down his cheeks. Venerable Ananda asked him, "Friend, why are you crying? Has your meditation not been successful? Do you have some regret?" The layman Anathapindika replied, "Venerable Ananda, I do not regret anything. The meditation has been most successful. I am crying because I am so deeply moved. I have been fortunate to have been able to serve the Buddha and his community for many years, yet I have never heard a teaching so wonderful and precious as the teaching transmitted by the Venerable Shariputra today."

Then the Venerable Ananda said to the layman Anathapindika, "Do you not know, friend, that the Buddha often gives this teaching to bhikshus and bhikshunis?" The layman Anathapindika replied, "Venerable Ananda, please tell the Buddha that there are also laypeople with the capacity to listen, understand, and put into practice these deep and wonderful teachings."

After listening to and practicing with the two venerable monks, Anathapindika felt free and at ease, and gave rise to the highest mind. The Venerables Shariputra and Ananda bade him farewell and went back to the monastery, and Anathapindika passed away and was born in the thirty-third heaven.

4. CONTEMPLATION ON NO-COMING AND NO-GOING ♪

This body is not me.
I am not limited by this body.
I am life without boundaries.
I have never been born,
and I have never died.
Look at the ocean and the sky filled with stars,
manifestations from my wondrous True Mind.
Since before time, I have been free.
Birth and death are only doors through which we pass,
sacred thresholds on our journey.
Birth and death are a game of hide-and-seek.
So laugh with me,
hold my hand,
let us say good-bye,
say good-bye, to meet again soon.

We meet today.
We will meet again tomorrow.
We will meet at the source every moment.
We meet each other in all forms of life.
[BELL]

5. MINDFULNESS OF LOVED ONES

Brothers and Sisters, it is time to bring our loved ones to mind: those to whom we wish to send the healing energy of love and compassion. Let us sit and enjoy our breathing for a few moments, allowing our beloved ones to be present with us now.

[TEN BREATHS IN SILENCE]

Please listen carefully: a moment of deep peace can light up the whole world. We have gathered today to awaken inner peace in each of us. Thanks to sitting and walking meditation, and chanting the name of the Bodhisattva Avalokiteshvara, we can establish communion with her energy of love and no-fear, which can transform the situation.

The peace and happiness of the world depend on our peace and happiness in this moment. Let us concentrate in order to invoke the names of the Bodhisattva Avalokiteshvara.

Namo'valokiteshvaraya ♪
[repeat nine times]
[BELL, BELL]

6. BEGINNING ANEW

I, your disciple
with my heart at peace and pure,
join my palms as a lotus bud
and turn respectfully to you
the great hero of loving kindness,
and conqueror of afflictions, Shakyamuni Buddha,
as I offer words of fervent repentance. [BELL]

I was not fortunate enough
to bring the teachings into my life earlier
and so lived in forgetfulness for a long time.
Obscured by ignorance, I have brought about suffering
and have made many foolish mistakes.
I and my ancestors
have sown our heart's garden with unwholesome seeds.
We have been responsible for killing, stealing,
sexual misconduct, and wrong speech.
Much of what we have said and done
has continued to do damage day after day.
I repent of these countless afflictions
that have obstructed my happiness.
I vow to begin anew from today. [BELL]

I see I have been thoughtless
and wandered from the path of mindfulness.
Ignorance and afflictions have accumulated in me
and created feelings of hatred and grief.
My mind is sometimes weary of life
and troubled by anxiety.
Because I have not understood others
I have been angry and resentful,
arguing and blaming,
courting suffering everyday,
making greater the rift between us.
There are days when we do not want
to speak to or look at each other,
and the internal knots last a long time.
Now I turn to the Three Jewels.
In sincere repentance I bow my head. [BELL]

I know that in my consciousness
are buried countless wholesome seeds of love and understanding,
and of peace and joy.
But because I have not known how to water them
the wholesome seeds have not sprouted fresh and green.
Overwhelmed by suffering
I have made my life dark.

I have grown used to chasing a distant happiness.
My mind is constantly occupied by the past
or travelling far into the future.
I am caught in a cycle of anger.
Unable to appreciate the precious things I have,
I trample on real happiness,
so suffering is there month after month, year after year.
Now before the altar, fragrant with incense
I vow to change and begin anew. [BELL]

With sincerity and respect,
I turn to the buddhas in the ten directions
and the bodhisattvas, the hearer disciples,
self-awakened buddhas, and the holy ones.
With deep regret I repent my repeated mistakes.
May the nectar of purity
extinguish the flames of my afflictions.
May the boat of the true Dharma
carry me out of resentment.
I vow to live in an awakened way,
to train according to the true teachings that have been transmitted.
I vow to practice mindful breathing and smiling
and diligently live in mindfulness. [BELL]

I vow to come back to myself
and live in the wonderful present moment,
to sow wholesome seeds in my heart's garden,
cultivating understanding and love.
I vow to learn to look deeply
and practice deep understanding,
to see the true nature of all that is
and free myself from the suffering
brought about by the notion of birth and death.
I vow to practice loving speech,
to love and care for others throughout the day,
bringing the source of joy to many places,
helping people to suffer less,
and repaying the deep gratitude I owe
to parents, teachers, and friends.

With faith I light up the incense of my heart.
I turn to the Compassionate One
and ask for protection on the wonderful path of practice.
I vow to train myself diligently
so that the fruits of the path can ripen.
[BELL, BELL]

7. THE THREE REFUGES ♪

I take refuge in the Buddha,
the one who shows me the way in this life.
I take refuge in the Dharma,
the way of understanding and of love.
I take refuge in the Sangha,
the community that lives in harmony and awareness.
[BELL]

Dwelling in the refuge of Buddha,
I clearly see the path of light and beauty in the world.
Dwelling in the refuge of Dharma,
I learn to open many doors on the path of transformation.
Dwelling in the refuge of Sangha,
shining light that supports me, keeping my practice free of obstruction.
[BELL]

Taking refuge in the Buddha in myself,
I aspire to help all people recognize their own awakened nature,
realizing the Mind of Love.
Taking refuge in the Dharma in myself,
I aspire to help all people fully master the ways of practice
and walk together on the path of liberation.
Taking refuge in the Sangha in myself,
I aspire to help all people build Fourfold Communities,
to embrace all beings and support their transformation.
[BELL, BELL]

8. SHARING THE MERIT ♪

Reciting the sutras, practicing the way of awareness
gives rise to benefits without limit.
We vow to share the fruits with all beings.
We vow to offer tribute to parents, teachers, friends,
and numerous beings
who give guidance and support along the path.
[BELL]
May all be born in the Pure Land.
As the lotus blooms,
may we realize the truth of no-birth and no-death.
May buddhas and bodhisattvas be our companions
on the path of practice. [Bell]
May we end all afflictions
so that understanding can arise,
the obstacles of unwholesome acts be dissolved,
and the fruit of awakening be fully realized. [BELL, BELL, BELL]

9. WORDS OF GRATITUDE

[At this time, a relative or friend of the dying person is invited to come mindfully before the community to offer a few words of gratitude to everyone who participated in the ceremony.]

Ceremony for Consecrating Water ॐ

[This ceremony is used for consecrating water when monks and nuns are ordained or when a new altar, school, house, plot of land, business, doctor's office, etc., is to be blessed. To give the ceremony meaning, we rely on Avalokiteshvara's great compassion for the water to become the nectar that purifies, freshens, revives, and heals wherever it is sprinkled..

Avalokiteshvara is the bodhisattva of great compassion who has the capacity to listen deeply to others and out of that understanding to relieve their suffering. In all of us the nature of that bodhisattva can be found.

A bowl of clear water and a leafy willow branch or a small flower with many petals are needed. Clear water symbolizes the power of concentration, and the willow branch or flower symbolizes wisdom.]

1. INTRODUCTORY VERSE

On the tip of the willow branch is the supreme nectar.
When one drop falls, it fills the ten directions
and puts an end to countless afflictions.
Our place of practice here is purified.
Homage to the Bodhisattva who refreshes the earth.
[BELL]

2. PRAISING THE BODHISATTVA OF COMPASSION

The nectar of compassion is seen on the willow branch
held by the Bodhisattva.
A single drop of this nectar is enough to bring life
to the ten directions of the cosmos.
May all afflictions of this world disappear
and may this place of practice be completely purified
by the Bodhisattva's nectar of compassion.
Homage to the Bodhisattva who refreshes the earth.
[BELL]

3. FROM THE DEPTHS OF UNDERSTANDING ♪

From the depths of understanding, a flower of great eloquence blooms:
The Bodhisattva stands majestically
upon the waves of birth and death, free from all afflictions.
Her great compassion eliminates all sickness,
even that once thought of as incurable.
Her wondrous light sweeps away all obstacles and dangers.
Her willow branch, once waved,
reveals countless buddha lands.
Her lotus flower blossoms a multitude of practice centers.
We bow to her. We see her true presence in the here and the now.
We offer her the incense of our hearts.
May the Bodhisattva of Deep Listening embrace us all
with great compassion.
Namo 'valokitesvaraya

4. VERSES OF CONSECRATION

From the willow branch, the clear water of compassion
falls on all three chiliocosms.
Its empty nature and its eight virtues
are the salvation of gods and men.
They make the Dharma realms brighter and more expansive.
They put an end to animosity and anger,
changing a blazing fire into a cool lotus lake.
Homage to the Bodhisattva who refreshes the earth.
[BELL, BELL]

Holding the willow branch,
you sprinkle the nectar of compassion and
destroy heat, cooling and refreshing the world.
You listen deeply in order to help those who suffer
and relieve their pain by bringing the wonderful Dharma.
Your compassion is unshakable.
Your presence brings freedom and serenity.
You respond wherever there is a need,
never failing those who appeal for your help.

Now we, your disciples, with right faith and a calm mind,
recite the verse for consecrating water.
[BELL]

[The head of ceremony raises up the bowl of clear water with the left hand and forms the mudra of peace with the right hand at the level of the forehead, and then chants aloud to consecrate the water. The assembled community follows their breathing to establish concentration.]

This water's shape is round or square
according to the container that holds it.
It is high or low according to the temperature of the season.
In the spring warmth, it is liquid; in the winter cold, it is solid.
When its path is open, it flows.
When its path is obstructed, it stands still.
How vast it is, yet its source is so small it is difficult to find.
How wonderful it is in its streams which flow endlessly.
In the jade rivulets, the footprints of dragons remain.
In the deep pond, water holds the bright halo
of the autumn moon.
On the tip of the king's pen,
water becomes the compassion of clemency.
On the willow branch of the Bodhisattva,
it becomes the clear fresh balm of compassion.
Only one drop of this water is needed,
and the ten directions are all purified.
[BELL]

5. RECITATION OF BODHISATTVA AVALOKITESHVARA'S NAME ♪

[During the recitation of the Bodhisattva's name, the purified water is sprinkled with the willow branch or flower over the head of the ordinee, or around the perimeter of the hall or building to be consecrated.]
Brothers and sisters, with one-pointed concentration please chant the name of Avalokiteshvara:
Namo 'valokitesvaraya
[Repeat twenty-one times]
[BELL]

6. SHARING THE MERIT ♪

Reciting the sutras, practicing the way of awareness
gives rise to benefits without limit.
We vow to share the fruits with all beings.
We vow to offer tribute to parents, teachers, friends,
and numerous beings
who give guidance and support along the path.
[BELL, BELL, BELL]

7. WORDS OF GRATITUDE BY HOST (OPTIONAL)

*[At this time, the host is invited to come mindfully before the community to offer
a few words of gratitude to everyone who participated in the ceremony.]*

Ceremony for Closing the Coffin or Cremation ॐ

[This ceremony is to pay last respects to the deceased and close the coffin.

During this ceremony, consecrated water symbolizing the nectar of compassion is sprinkled on and around the coffin for the sangha to give rise to the energy of calm and compassion. A bowl of clear water and a branch of willow or a small flower with many petals are needed. The clear water symbolizes the power of concentration, and the branch of green willow or flower symbolizes deep understanding.]

1. OPENING VERSE ♪

[BELL, BELL, BELL]
Namo Tassa Bhagavato Arahato Samma Sambuddhassa
Namo Tassa Bhagavato Arahato Samma Sambuddhassa
Namo Tassa Bhagavato Arahato Samma Sambuddhassa
[BELL]
The Dharma is deep and lovely.
We now have a chance to see, study, and practice it.
We vow to realize its true meaning.
[BELL]

2. INTRODUCTORY WORDS

[Spoken by the head of ceremony. You can adapt the words to the situation]

Dear friends, today we have gathered here to bless the corpse of [name of deceased] with the pure water of compassion and our chanting, in the presence of the children, the family, the friends and relatives of the deceased. We are aware that this is a chance to offer together our love and our spiritual support at this important moment of transformation.

Dear friends, please listen:
The parents and grandparents, whether they are still alive or have passed away are always present in their children, grandchildren, and dear ones.

Our life is their life. Our life continues their life. According to the teachings of the Awakened One, our peace and happiness are their peace and happiness. As we keep our mind pure and peaceful, we create the condition for the peace and happiness of our parents and our grandparents. The peace and happiness of [name of the deceased] depend on our peace and happiness in this moment. Let us concentrate as we chant for our loved one.

3. CONTEMPLATION ON NO-COMING AND NO-GOING ♪

This body is not me.
I am not limited by this body.
I am life without boundaries.
I have never been born,
and I have never died.
Look at the ocean and the sky filled with stars,
manifestations from my wondrous true mind.
Since before time, I have been free.
Birth and death are only doors through which we pass,
sacred thresholds on our journey.
Birth and death are a game of hide-and-seek.
So laugh with me,
hold my hand,
let us say good-bye,
say good-bye, to meet again soon.
We meet today.
We will meet again tomorrow.
We will meet at the source every moment.
We meet each other in all forms of life.
[BELL]

4. VERSES OF CONSECRATION

[The head of ceremony raises up the bowl of clear water with the left hand and forms the mudra of peace with the right hand at the level of the forehead, and then reads or chants aloud to consecrate the water. Members of the community follow their breathing, listening with ease and concentration.]

[READ OR CHANTED BY HEAD OF CEREMONY]
This water, by its nature, is endowed with the eight qualities.

It washes away the dust and impurities of all living beings,
leading them all into the wonderful Avatamsaka World.
May all beings without exception overcome their suffering.
Water does not wash water,
that is the wonderful Dharma body.
Dust does not cling to dust—
the mind opens naturally.
Once the water is sprinkled
this place of practice is purified.
The wilting plant grows fresh and green again,
the world of defilement changes into a world of purity,
and all beings are refreshed and can live in peace and joy.
Homage to the Bodhisattva who refreshes the earth.
[BELL]

The Tao Khe stream is jade in color,
flowing always towards the east.
Avalokiteshvara's vase of pure water
washes clean the traces of worldly dust.
The willow branch sprinkles the nectar of compassion,
reviving the spring season.
The nectar that soothes thirst and hunger,
calms hearts.
Homage to the Bodhisattva of the nectar of compassion.
Homage to the Bodhisattva of the nectar of compassion.
Homage to the Bodhisattva of the nectar of compassion.
[BELL]

The nectar of compassion is seen on the willow branch
held by the Bodhisattva.
A single drop of this nectar fills
the ten directions of the cosmos.
May all afflictions of this world disappear,
and may this place of practice be purified.
Homage to the Bodhisattva who refreshes the earth
Homage to the Bodhisattva who refreshes the earth
Homage to the Bodhisattva who refreshes the earth
[BELL]

5. May the Day Be Well ♪

[This is chanted as the body of the deceased and the coffin are sprinkled with consecrated water.]

May the day be well and the night be well.
May the midday hour bring happiness too.
In every minute and every second,
may the day and night be well.
By the blessing of the Triple Gem,
may all things be protected and safe.
May all beings born in each of the four ways
live in a land of purity.
May all in the three realms be born upon lotus thrones.
May countless wandering souls
realize the three virtuous positions of the bodhisattva path.
May all living beings, with grace and ease,
fulfill the bodhisattva stages.
The countenance of the World-Honored One, like the full moon
or like the orb of the sun, shines with the light of clarity.
A halo of wisdom spreads in every direction,
enveloping all with love and compassion,
joy and equanimity.
Namo Shakyamunaye Buddhaya
Namo Shakyamunaye Buddhaya
Namo Shakyamunaye Buddhaya
[BELL, BELL]

6. Invocation of the Buddhas and Bodhisattvas

[Read or chanted by head of ceremony]

The river of attachment is unending.
There are countless waves on the ocean of ignorance.
If you wish to be free from the world of birth and death,
recollect the Buddha with a one-pointed mind.

[As the chanting continues, the assembled community can optionally circum-ambulate the coffin, paying their last respects and offering flowers and gifts. The

chanting is concluded when everyone has had the chance to pay their final re-
spects, and the coffin is then closed.]

Recitation ♪
[All chant each name three times]
Om Namo Shakyamunaye Buddhaya
[Homage to Shakyamuni Buddha, the Fully Awakened One]
[BELL]

Om Namo 'mitabhaya Buddhaya
[Homage the Buddha of Infinite Light]
[BELL]

Om Namo Manjushriye Bodhisattvaya
[Homage to Manjushri, Bodhisattva of Great Understanding]
[BELL]

Om Namo Samantabhadraya Bodhisattvaya
[Homage to Samantabhadra, Bodhisattva of Great Action]
[BELL]

Om Namo 'valokitesvaraya Bodhisattvaya
[Homage to Avalokiteshvara, Bodhisattva of Great Compassion]
[BELL]

Om Namo Kshitigarbha ya Bodhisattvaya
[Homage to Kshitigarbha, Bodhisattva of Great Aspiration]
[BELL]

7. THE THREE REFUGES ♪

I take refuge in the Buddha,
the one who shows me the way in this life.
I take refuge in the Dharma,
the way of understanding and of love.
I take refuge in the Sangha,
the community that lives in harmony and awareness.
[BELL]

Dwelling in the refuge of Buddha,
I clearly see the path of light and beauty in the world.
Dwelling in the refuge of Dharma,
I learn to open many doors on the path of transformation.
Dwelling in the refuge of Sangha,
shining light that supports me, keeping my practice free of obstruction.
[BELL]

Taking refuge in the Buddha in myself,
I aspire to help all people recognize their own awakened nature,
realizing the mind of love.
Taking refuge in the Dharma in myself,
I aspire to help all people fully master the ways of practice
and walk together on the path of liberation.
Taking refuge in the Sangha in myself,
I aspire to help all people build fourfold communities,
to embrace all beings and support their transformation.
[BELL, BELL]

8. Sharing the Merit, *Pure Land Version* ♪

Reciting the sutras, practicing the way of awareness
gives rise to benefits without limit.
We vow to share the fruits with all beings.
We vow to offer tribute to parents, teachers, friends,
and numerous beings
who give guidance and support along the path.
[BELL]

May all be born in the Pure Land.
As the lotus blooms,
may we realize the truth of no-birth and no-death.
May buddhas and bodhisattvas be our companions
on the path of practice.
[BELL]

May we end all afflictions
so that understanding can arise,

the obstacles of unwholesome acts be dissolved,
and the fruit of awakening be fully realized.
[BELL, BELL, BELL]

(Friends and relatives of the deceased can at this point offer a song or eulogy recalling the qualities and accomplishments of the deceased.)

9. HUGGING MEDITATION
(Spoken by the head of ceremony)

Dear friends, throughout this ceremony we have seen that our own peace and joy are the peace and joy of our loved one who has died. In order to express our gratitude and love for [name of deceased], their relatives and friends are invited to turn to each other, to look deeply at each other as they breathe mindfully. Look each other in the eyes, accept and forgive each other; recognize that to be alive is a true miracle. If you are aware of that truth, your heart will be full of love, acceptance, and forgiveness. Hold each other in your arms and breathe peacefully three times to feel the real presence of your friend, or relative who is still alive in your arms. Your harmony, peace, and joy are the most precious gift you can offer to [name of deceased].

Let the whole community remain mindful in order to support our friends who are practicing hugging meditation.

Ceremony for the Deceased ॐ

[This ceremony can be used when we hear of the decease of a loved one, or when we wish to commemorate the anniversary of the decease of a loved one. Traditionally, this ceremony is also used on the one-hundredth day after decease.

A photograph of the deceased can be placed on the ancestral altar with a small placard on which are written their name and the dates of birth and passing away. Optionally an offering of food can be made to the deceased and placed on the ancestral altar in front of their photograph. The food should be something that the deceased enjoyed during their lifetime.

Ceremonies for the deceased can be adapted to suit the circumstances as well as local customs and traditions.]

1. Walking Meditation Outdoors (optional)

2. Sitting Meditation [12 minutes]

3. Incense Offering ♪
[BELL BELL BELL]

In gratitude, we offer this incense
throughout space and time
to all buddhas and bodhisattvas.
May it be fragrant as earth herself,
reflecting careful efforts,
wholehearted awareness,
and the fruit of understanding
slowly ripening.
May we and all beings
be companions of buddhas and bodhisattvas.
May we awaken from forgetfulness
and realize our true home.
[BELL]

4. TOUCHING THE EARTH ♪

Introductory Verse
The one who bows and the one who is bowed to
are both, by nature, empty.
Therefore the communication between them
is inexpressibly perfect.
Our practice center is the net of Indra
reflecting all buddhas everywhere.
And with my person in front of each buddha,
I go with my whole life for refuge.
[BELL]

Touching the Earth
[Touch the earth one time at the sound of each bell.]
Offering light in the ten directions,
the Buddha, the Dharma, and the Sangha,
to whom we bow in gratitude.
[BELL]

Teaching and living the way of awareness
in the very midst of suffering and confusion,
Shakyamuni Buddha, the Fully Enlightened One,
to whom we bow in gratitude.
[BELL]

Cutting through ignorance, awakening our hearts and our minds,
Manjushri, the Bodhisattva of Great Understanding,
to whom we bow in gratitude.
[BELL]
Working mindfully, working joyfully for the sake of all beings,
Samantabhadra, the Bodhisattva of Great Action,
to whom we bow in gratitude.
[BELL]

Listening deeply, serving beings in countless ways,
Avalokiteshvara, the Bodhisattva of Great Compassion,
to whom we bow in gratitude.
[BELL]

Fearless and persevering through realms of suffering and darkness,
Kshitigarbha, the Bodhisattva of Great Aspiration,
to whom we bow in gratitude.
[BELL]

Mother of buddhas, bodhisattvas, and all beings, nourishing,
holding, and healing all, Bodhisattva Gaia, Great Mother Earth,
precious jewel of the cosmos, to whom we bow in gratitude.
[BELL]

Radiating light in all directions, source of life on earth,
Mahavairocana Tathagata, Great Father Sun, Buddha of Infinite
Light and Life, to whom we bow in gratitude.
[BELL]

Showing the way fearlessly and compassionately,
the stream of all our ancestral teachers,
to whom we bow in gratitude.
[BELL, BELL]

5. OPENING VERSE ♪

Namo Tassa Bhagavato Arahato Samma Sambuddhassa
Namo Tassa Bhagavato Arahato Samma Sambuddhassa
Namo Tassa Bhagavato Arahato Samma Sambuddhassa
[BELL]

The Dharma is deep and lovely.
We now have a chance to see, study, and practice it.
We vow to realize its true meaning.
[BELL]

6. THE SUTRA OF THE INSIGHT THAT BRINGS US TO THE OTHER SHORE ♪

Avalokiteshvara, while practicing deeply
with the insight that brings us to the other shore,
suddenly discovered that all of the five skandhas are equally empty,

and with this realization he overcame all ill-being. [BELL]
"Listen Shariputra, this body itself is emptiness
and emptiness itself is this body.
This body is not other than emptiness
and emptiness is not other than this body.
The same is true of feelings, perceptions,
mental formations, and consciousness. [BELL]

"Listen Shariputra, all phenomena bear the mark of emptiness;
their true nature is the nature of no birth no death,
no being no nonbeing, no defilement no purity,
no increasing no decreasing. [BELL]

"That is why in emptiness, body, feelings,
perceptions, mental formations, and consciousness
are not separate self-entities.
The eighteen realms of phenomena, which are the six sense organs,
six sense objects, and six consciousnesses
are also not separate self-entities.
The Twelve Links of Interdependent Arising
and their extinction are also not separate self-entities.
Ill-being, the causes of ill-being,
the end of ill-being, the path, insight, and attainment,
are also not separate self-entities.
Whoever can see this
no longer needs anything to attain. [BELL]

"Bodhisattvas who practice the insight that brings us to the
other shore
see no more obstacles in their mind,
and because there are no more obstacles in their mind,
they can overcome all fear, destroy all wrong perceptions,
and realize perfect nirvana. [BELL]

"All buddhas in the past, present, and future
by practicing the insight that brings us to the other shore
are all capable of attaining authentic and perfect
enlightenment. [BELL]

"Therefore Shariputra, it should be known that
the insight that brings us to the other shore is a great mantra,
the most illuminating mantra, the highest mantra,
a mantra beyond compare,
the true wisdom that has the power
to put an end to all kinds of suffering. [BELL]

"Therefore let us proclaim a mantra
to praise the insight that brings us to the other shore
Gate gate paragate parasamgate bodhi svaha!
Gate gate paragate parasamgate bodhi svaha!
Gate gate paragate parasamgate bodhi svaha!"
[BELL BELL]

7. INTRODUCTORY WORDS
[Adapt as appropriate]

Today the community has gathered to recite the sutras, to invoke the Buddhas' and Bodhisattvas' names, and to offer the merit for [name of deceased]. The children, relatives, and friends of [name of deceased] are here to take part in the ceremony.

We ask the community to listen with a quiet mind. Parents and grandparents, whether they are still alive or have left this life, are present in their children and grandchildren. The life of children and grandchildren is the life of the parents and the grandparents. The life of the ancestors carries on in the life of the children and grandchildren. According to the teaching of the Buddha, the peace and joy of the children and grandchildren are the peace and joy of the parents, grandparents, and all ancestors. With a feeling of calm, clarity, and peace, we will make possible the calm, clarity, and peace of those who have left this life.

[OPTIONAL: Please will the children, grandchildren, and close relatives of [name of deceased] stand before the Three Jewels, join your palms and touch the earth to the Buddhas and Bodhisattvas.]

8. Touching the Earth ♪

[Recited by head of ceremony as relatives touch the earth]

Offering light in the ten directions,
the Buddha, the Dharma, and the Sangha,
to whom we bow in gratitude.
[BELL]

Teaching and living the way of awareness
in the very midst of suffering and confusion,
Shakyamuni Buddha, the Fully Enlightened One,
to whom we bow in gratitude.
[BELL]

Cutting through ignorance, awakening our hearts and our minds,
Manjushri, the Bodhisattva of Great Understanding,
to whom we bow in gratitude.
[BELL]

Working mindfully, working joyfully for the sake of all beings,
Samantabhadra, the Bodhisattva of Great Action,
to whom we bow in gratitude.
[BELL]

Listening deeply, serving beings in countless ways,
Avalokiteshvara, the Bodhisattva of Great Compassion,
to whom we bow in gratitude.
[BELL]

Fearless and persevering through realms of suffering and darkness,
Kshitigarbha, the Bodhisattva of Great Aspiration,
to whom we bow in gratitude.
[BELL]

Showing the way fearlessly and compassionately,
the stream of all our ancestral teachers,
to whom we bow in gratitude.
[BELL, BELL]

9. CONTEMPLATION ON NO-COMING, NO-GOING ♪

This body is not me.
I am not limited by this body.
I am life without boundaries.
I have never been born,
and I have never died.

Look at the ocean and the sky filled with stars,
manifestations from my wondrous true mind.

Since before time, I have been free.
Birth and death are only doors through which we pass,
sacred thresholds on our journey.
Birth and death are a game of hide-and-seek.

So laugh with me,
hold my hand,
let us say good-bye,
say good-bye, to meet again soon.

We meet today.
We will meet again tomorrow.
We will meet at the source every moment.
We meet each other in all forms of life.
[BELL]

10. INVOCATION OF THE BUDDHAS AND BODHISATTVAS

Introductory Verse
[Read by head of ceremony]
Brothers and sisters, please listen. The peace and joy of the entire world, including the worlds of the living and the dead, depend upon our own peace and joy in this moment. With all our heart and one-pointed mind, we recite the names of the buddhas and bodhisattvas.
The river of attachment is unending.
There are countless waves on the ocean of ignorance.
If you wish to be free from the world of birth and death,
recollect the Buddha with a one-pointed mind.

Recitation ♪
[All chant each name three times]

Om Namo Shakyamunaye Buddhaya
[Homage to Shakyamuni Buddha, the Fully Awakened One]
[BELL]

Om Namo 'mitabhaya Buddhaya
[Homage to the Buddha of Infinite Light]
[BELL]

Namo Manjushriye Bodhisattvaya
[Homage to Manjushri, Bodhisattva of Great Understanding]
[BELL]

Namo Samantabhadraya Bodhisattvaya
[Homage to Samantabhadra, Bodhisattva of Great Action]
[BELL]

Namo 'valokiteshvaraya Bodhisattvaya
[Homage to Avalokiteshvara Bodhisattva of Great Compassion]
[BELL]

Namo Kshitigarbhaya Bodhisattvaya
[Homage to Kshitigarbha, Bodhisattva of Great Aspiration]
[BELL, BELL]

11. BEGINNING ANEW (ON BEHALF OF THE DECEASED AND THOSE WHO ARE RECITING)

I, your disciple
with my heart at peace and pure,
join my palms as a lotus bud
and turn respectfully to you
the great hero of loving kindness,
and conqueror of afflictions, Shakyamuni Buddha,
as I offer words of fervent repentance. [BELL]

I was not fortunate enough
to bring the teachings into my life earlier

and so lived in forgetfulness for a long time.
Obscured by ignorance, I have brought about suffering
and have made many foolish mistakes.
I and my ancestors
have sown our heart's garden with unwholesome seeds.
We have been responsible for killing, stealing,
sexual misconduct, and wrong speech.
Much of what we have said and done
has continued to do damage day after day.
I repent of these countless afflictions
that have obstructed my happiness.
I vow to begin anew from today. [BELL]

I see I have been thoughtless
and wandered from the path of mindfulness.
Ignorance and afflictions have accumulated in me
and created feelings of hatred and grief.
My mind is sometimes weary of life
and troubled by anxiety.
Because I have not understood others
I have been angry and resentful,
arguing and blaming,
courting suffering everyday,
making greater the rift between us.
There are days when we do not want
to speak to or look at each other,
and the internal knots last a long time.
Now I turn to the Three Jewels.
In sincere repentance I bow my head. [BELL]

I know that in my consciousness
are buried countless wholesome seeds of love and understanding,
and of peace and joy.
But because I have not known how to water them
the wholesome seeds have not sprouted fresh and green.
Overwhelmed by suffering
I have made my life dark.
I have grown used to chasing a distant happiness.
My mind is constantly occupied by the past
or travelling far into the future.

I am caught in a cycle of anger.
Unable to appreciate the precious things I have,
I trample on real happiness,
so suffering is there month after month, year after year.
Now before the altar, fragrant with incense
I vow to change and begin anew. [BELL]

With sincerity and respect,
I turn to the buddhas in the ten directions
and the bodhisattvas, the hearer disciples,
self-awakened buddhas, and the holy ones.
With deep regret I repent my repeated mistakes.
May the nectar of purity
extinguish the flames of my afflictions.
May the boat of the true Dharma
carry me out of resentment.
I vow to live in an awakened way,
to train according to the true teachings that have been transmitted.
I vow to practice mindful breathing and smiling
and diligently live in mindfulness. [BELL]

I vow to come back to myself
and live in the wonderful present moment,
to sow wholesome seeds in my heart's garden,
cultivating understanding and love.
I vow to learn to look deeply
and practice deep understanding,
to see the true nature of all that is
and free myself from the suffering
brought about by the notion of birth and death.
I vow to practice loving speech,
to love and care for others throughout the day,
bringing the source of joy to many places,
helping people to suffer less,
and repaying the deep gratitude I owe
to parents, teachers, and friends.
With faith I light up the incense of my heart.
I turn to the Compassionate One
and ask for protection on the wonderful path of practice.

I vow to train myself diligently
so that the fruits of the path can ripen.
[BELL, BELL]

12. EULOGIES FOR THE DECEASED

13. SILENT CONTEMPLATION (5 MINUTES)

Brothers and sisters, let us now sit in silence to concentrate on all the virtuous qualities of the deceased, with our mind at peace.

14. [APPROPRIATE OFFERINGS OF SONGS AND MUSIC CHOSEN BY THE RELATIVES]

15. THE THREE REFUGES ♪

I take refuge in the Buddha,
the one who shows me the way in this life.
I take refuge in the Dharma,
the way of understanding and of love.
I take refuge in the Sangha,
the community that lives in harmony and awareness.
[BELL]

Dwelling in the refuge of Buddha,
I clearly see the path of light and beauty in the world.
Dwelling in the refuge of Dharma,
I learn to open many doors on the path of transformation.
Dwelling in the refuge of Sangha,
shining light that supports me, keeping my practice free of obstruction.
[BELL]

Taking refuge in the Buddha in myself,
I aspire to help all people recognize their own awakened nature,
realizing the Mind of Love.
Taking refuge in the Dharma in myself,
I aspire to help all people fully master the ways of practice
and walk together on the path of liberation.
Taking refuge in the Sangha in myself,

I aspire to help all people build Fourfold Communities,
to embrace all beings and support their transformation.
[BELL, BELL]

16. SHARING THE MERIT, PURE LAND VERSION ♪

Reciting the sutras, practicing the way of awareness
gives rise to benefits without limit.
We vow to share the fruits with all beings.
We vow to offer tribute to parents, teachers, friends,
and numerous beings
who give guidance and support along the path.
[BELL]

May all be born in the Pure Land.
As the lotus blooms,
may we realize the truth of no-birth and no-death.
May buddhas and bodhisattvas be our companions
on the path of practice.
[BELL]

May we end all afflictions
so that understanding can arise,
the obstacles of unwholesome acts be dissolved,
and the fruit of awakening be fully realized.
[BELL, BELL, BELL]

17. WORDS OF GRATITUDE

[At this time, a relative or friend of the deceased is invited to come before the community and to offer a few words of gratitude to everyone who participated in the ceremony.]

18. LOOKING WITH THE EYES OF COMPASSION.

Throughout the ceremony today, we have been reminded that our peace and joy is the peace and joy of our loved one. In order to show gratitude and loyalty for the deceased, friends and relatives can stand before the ancestral altar, bow, and then turn to look at each other with the eyes of understanding, acceptance, and forgiveness. You can breathe mindfully three times while you practice this. Your peace and joy will be the foundation for the peace and joy of the deceased.

Ceremony for the Deceased on Every Seventh Day After the Decease until the Forty-Ninth Day ∞

[According to the belief in an intermediate state, those who have passed away can be reborn in a pure land as soon as they leave this life, or they can pass a period of time from one to seven weeks before being born in the pure land or taking rebirth. During that time, the body of the intermediate state passes through seven different transformations. We can generate a great deal of energy and active support for these transformations through the daily practice, reciting the sutras, generosity, and other meritorious acts. Every seven days, chanting of the sutra, invoking the names of buddhas and bodhisattvas, releasing birds and fish from captivity, and making offerings can be organized.

The ceremony can be supplemented by the reading of one of the discourses, such as "The Discourse on Love," "The Discourse on Happiness," "The Anuradha Discourse," "The Eight Realizations of Great Beings," "The Diamond that Cuts through Illusion," and "The Discourse on the White-Clad Disciple."

For each of the seventh-day ceremonies, a photograph of the deceased can be placed on the ancestral altar with a small placard on which are written their name and the dates of birth and passing away. For the "final seven" ceremony, an offering of food can be made to the deceased and placed on the ancestral altar in front of their photograph. This food could be something that the deceased enjoyed during their lifetime.

Ceremonies for the deceased can be adapted to suit the circumstances as well as local customs and traditions.

1. WALKING MEDITATION OUTDOORS (OPTIONAL)

2. SITTING MEDITATION [12 MINUTES]

3. INCENSE OFFERING

[BELL, BELL, BELL]
In gratitude, we offer this incense
throughout space and time

to all buddhas and bodhisattvas.
May it be fragrant as earth herself,
reflecting careful efforts,
wholehearted awareness,
and the fruit of understanding
slowly ripening.
May we and all beings
be companions of buddhas and bodhisattvas.
May we awaken from forgetfulness
and realize our true home.
[BELL]

4. TOUCHING THE EARTH ♪

Introductory Verse
The one who bows and the one who is bowed to
are both, by nature, empty.
Therefore the communication between them
is inexpressibly perfect.
Our practice center is the net of Indra
reflecting all buddhas everywhere.
And with my person in front of each buddha,
I go with my whole life for refuge.
[BELL]

Touching the Earth
[Touch the earth one time at the sound of each bell.]
Offering light in the ten directions,
the Buddha, the Dharma, and the Sangha,
to whom we bow in gratitude.
[BELL]

Teaching and living the way of awareness
in the very midst of suffering and confusion,
Shakyamuni Buddha, the Fully Enlightened One,
to whom we bow in gratitude.
[BELL]

Cutting through ignorance, awakening our hearts and our minds,
Manjushri, the Bodhisattva of Great Understanding,
to whom we bow in gratitude.
[BELL]

Working mindfully, working joyfully for the sake of all beings,
Samantabhadra, the Bodhisattva of Great Action,
to whom we bow in gratitude.
[BELL]

Listening deeply, serving beings in countless ways,
Avalokiteshvara, the Bodhisattva of Great Compassion,
to whom we bow in gratitude.
[BELL]

Fearless and persevering through realms of suffering and darkness,
Kshitigarbha, the Bodhisattva of Great Aspiration,
to whom we bow in gratitude.
[BELL]

Mother of buddhas, bodhisattvas, and all beings, nourishing,
holding, and healing all, Bodhisattva Gaia, Great Mother Earth,
precious jewel of the cosmos, to whom we bow in gratitude.
[BELL]

Radiating light in all directions, source of life on earth,
Mahavairocana Tathagata, Great Father Sun, Buddha of Infinite
Light and Life, to whom we bow in gratitude.
[BELL]

Showing the way fearlessly and compassionately,
the stream of all our ancestral teachers,
to whom we bow in gratitude.
[BELL, BELL]

5. BEGINNING ANEW CHANT (ON BEHALF OF THE DECEASED AND THOSE WHO ARE RECITING)

I, your disciple
with my heart at peace and pure,
join my palms as a lotus bud
and turn respectfully to you
the great hero of loving kindness,
and conqueror of afflictions, Shakyamuni Buddha,
as I offer words of fervent repentance.
[BELL]

I was not fortunate enough
to bring the teachings into my life earlier
and so lived in forgetfulness for a long time.
Obscured by ignorance, I have brought about suffering
and have made many foolish mistakes.
I and my ancestors
have sown our heart's garden with unwholesome seeds.
We have been responsible for killing, stealing,
sexual misconduct, and wrong speech.
Much of what we have said and done
has continued to do damage day after day.
I repent of these countless afflictions
that have obstructed my happiness.
I vow to begin anew from today.
[BELL]

I see I have been thoughtless
and wandered from the path of mindfulness.
Ignorance and afflictions have accumulated in me
and created feelings of hatred and grief.
My mind is sometimes weary of life
and troubled by anxiety.
Because I have not understood others
I have been angry and resentful,
arguing and blaming,
courting suffering every day,

making greater the rift between us.
There are days when we do not want
to speak to or look at each other,
and the internal knots last a long time.
Now I turn to the Three Jewels.
In sincere repentance I bow my head.
[BELL]

I know that in my consciousness
are buried countless wholesome seeds of love and understanding
and of peace and joy.
But because I have not known how to water them
the wholesome seeds have not sprouted fresh and green.
Overwhelmed by suffering
I have made my life dark.
I have grown used to chasing a distant happiness.
My mind is constantly occupied by the past
or travelling far into the future.
I am caught in a cycle of anger.
Unable to appreciate the precious things I have,
I trample on real happiness,
so suffering is there month after month, year after year.
Now before the altar fragrant with incense,
I vow to change and begin anew.
[BELL]

With sincerity and respect,
I turn to the buddhas in the ten directions
and the bodhisattvas, the hearer disciples,
self-awakened buddhas, and the holy ones.
With deep regret I repent
the repeated mistakes I have made.
May the nectar of purity
extinguish the flames of my afflictions.
May the boat of the true Dharma
carry me out of resentment.
I vow to live in an awakened way,
To train according to the true teachings that have been transmitted
I vow to practice mindful breathing and smiling

and diligently live in mindfulness.
[BELL]

I vow to come back to myself
and live in the wonderful present moment,
to sow wholesome seeds in my heart's garden
cultivating understanding and love.
I vow to learn to look deeply
and practice deep understanding,
to see the true nature of all that is
and free myself from the suffering
brought about by the notion of birth and death.
I vow to practice loving speech,
to love and care for others throughout the day,
bringing the source of joy to many places,
helping people to suffer less,
and repaying the deep gratitude I owe
to parents, teachers, and friends.
With faith I light up the incense of my heart.
I turn to the Compassionate One
and ask for protection on the wonderful path of practice.
I vow to train myself diligently
so that the fruits of the path can ripen.
[BELL, BELL]

6. CONTEMPLATION ON NO-COMING, NO-GOING ♪

This body is not me.
I am not limited by this body.
I am life without boundaries.
I have never been born,
and I have never died.

Look at the ocean and the sky filled with stars,
manifestations from my wondrous True Mind.

Since before time, I have been free.
Birth and death are only doors through which we pass,

198 : CHANTING FROM THE HEART

sacred thresholds on our journey.
Birth and death are a game of hide-and-seek.

So laugh with me,
hold my hand,
let us say good-bye,
say good-bye, to meet again soon.

We meet today.
We will meet again tomorrow.
We will meet at the source every moment.
We meet each other in all forms of life.
[BELL]

7. SILENT CONTEMPLATION (5 MINUTES)

Brothers and sisters, we can meditate to see the continuation of the deceased in their children, grandchildren, and friends, as well as in the elements of earth, water, fire, air, space, and consciousness.

8. THE REFUGE CHANT ♪

Incense perfumes the atmosphere.
A lotus blooms and the Buddha appears.
The world of suffering and discrimination
is filled with the light of the rising sun.
As the dust of fear and anxiety settles,
with open heart, one-pointed mind,
I turn to the Three Jewels.
[BELL]

The Fully Enlightened One, beautifully seated, peaceful and smiling,
a living source of understanding and compassion,
to the Buddha I go for refuge.
[BELL]

The path of mindful living,
leading to healing, joy, and enlightenment, the way of peace,
to the Dharma I go for refuge.
[BELL]

The loving and supportive community of practice,
realizing harmony, awareness, and liberation,
to the Sangha I go for refuge.
[BELL]

I am aware that the Three Gems are within my heart.
I vow to realize them,
practicing mindful breathing and smiling,
looking deeply into things.
I vow to understand living beings and their suffering,
to cultivate compassion and loving kindness,
to practice joy and equanimity.
[BELL]

I vow to offer joy to one person in the morning,
to help relieve the grief of one person in the afternoon,
living simply and sanely with few possessions,
keeping my body healthy.
I vow to let go of all worries and anxiety
in order to be light and free.
[BELL]

I am aware that I owe so much
to my parents, teachers, friends, and all beings.
I vow to be worthy of their trust, to practice wholeheartedly
so that understanding and compassion will flower,
helping living beings be free from their suffering.
May the Buddha, the Dharma, and the Sangha
support my efforts.
[BELL, BELL]

9. THE THREE REFUGES ♪

I take refuge in the Buddha,
the one who shows me the way in this life.
I take refuge in the Dharma,
the way of understanding and of love.
I take refuge in the Sangha,
the community that lives in harmony and awareness.
[BELL]

Dwelling in the refuge of Buddha,
I clearly see the path of light and beauty in the world.
Dwelling in the refuge of Dharma,
I learn to open many doors on the path of transformation.
Dwelling in the refuge of Sangha,
shining light that supports me, keeping my practice free of obstruction.
[BELL]

Taking refuge in the Buddha in myself,
I aspire to help all people recognize their own awakened nature,
realizing the Mind of Love.
Taking refuge in the Dharma in myself,
I aspire to help all people fully master the ways of practice
and walk together on the path of liberation.
Taking refuge in the Sangha in myself,
I aspire to help all people build Fourfold Communities,
to embrace all beings and support their transformation.
[BELL, BELL]

10. SHARING THE MERIT *Pure Land Version*

Reciting the sutras, practicing the way of awareness
gives rise to benefits without limit.
We vow to share the fruits with all beings.
We vow to offer tribute to parents, teachers, friends,
and numerous beings
who give guidance and support along the path.
[BELL]

May all be born in the Pure Land.
As the lotus blooms,
may we realize the truth of no-birth and no-death.
May buddhas and bodhisattvas be our companions
on the path of practice.
[BELL]

May we end all afflictions
so that understanding can arise,

the obstacles of unwholesome acts be dissolved,
and the fruit of awakening be fully realized.
[BELL, BELL, BELL]

Ceremony to Begin Anew with Mother Earth ౨

[In this ceremony we are representing the human species in order to express our regret to and make our deep aspiration to Mother Earth.]

1. TEN MINUTES SILENT SITTING OR GUIDED MEDITATION

Breathing in, I am aware that this is my in-breath.
Breathing out, I am in touch with my out-breath.
In-breath.
Out-breath.

Breathing in, I am aware of my whole body.
Breathing out, I relax my whole body.
Aware of whole body.
Relaxing whole body.

Breathing in, I am in touch with life inside of me.
Breathing out, I am in touch with the wonders of life all around me.
Life inside of me.
The wonders of life all around me.

Breathing in, I am fully established in the here and now.
Breathing out, I am here for Mother Earth.
Fully established.
Here for mother earth.

Breathing in, I smile to mother earth inside of me.
Breathing out, I smile to mother earth all around me, holding, embracing, and carrying me.
I smile to mother earth inside of me.
I smile to mother earth all around me.
[BELL]

2. INCENSE OFFERING ♪

[BELL, BELL, BELL]
In gratitude, we offer this incense
throughout space and time
to all buddhas and bodhisattvas.
May it be fragrant as earth herself,
reflecting careful efforts,
wholehearted awareness,
and the fruit of understanding
slowly ripening.
May we and all beings
be companions of buddhas and bodhisattvas.
May we awaken from forgetfulness
and realize our true home.
[BELL]

3. TOUCHING THE EARTH ♪

Introductory Verse ♪
The one who bows and the one who is bowed to
are both, by nature, empty.
Therefore the communication between them
is inexpressibly perfect.
Our practice center is the net of Indra
reflecting all buddhas everywhere.
And with my person in front of each buddha,
I go with my whole life for refuge.
[BELL]

TOUCHING THE EARTH ♪

Touching the Earth
[Touch the earth one time at the sound of each bell.]
Offering light in the ten directions,
the Buddha, the Dharma, and the Sangha,
to whom we bow in gratitude.
[BELL]

Teaching and living the way of awareness
in the very midst of suffering and confusion,
Shakyamuni Buddha, the Fully Enlightened One,
to whom we bow in gratitude.
[BELL]

Cutting through ignorance, awakening our hearts and our minds,
Manjushri, the Bodhisattva of Great Understanding,
to whom we bow in gratitude.
[BELL]

Working mindfully, working joyfully for the sake of all beings,
Samantabhadra, the Bodhisattva of Great Action,
to whom we bow in gratitude.
[BELL]

Listening deeply, serving beings in countless ways,
Avalokiteshvara, the Bodhisattva of Great Compassion,
to whom we bow in gratitude.
[BELL]

Fearless and persevering through realms of suffering and darkness,
Kshitigarbha, the Bodhisattva of Great Aspiration,
to whom we bow in gratitude.
[BELL]

Mother of buddhas, bodhisattvas, and all beings, nourishing,
holding, and healing all, Bodhisattva Gaia, Great Mother Earth,
precious jewel of the cosmos, to whom we bow in gratitude.
[BELL]

Radiating light in all directions, source of life on earth,
Mahavairocana Tathagata, Great Father Sun, Buddha of Infinite
Light and Life, to whom we bow in gratitude.
[BELL]

Showing the way fearlessly and compassionately,
the stream of all our ancestral teachers,
to whom we bow in gratitude.
[BELL, BELL]

4. BEGINNING ANEW CHANT

[One person reads, or everyone reads together]
We, your children
with our hearts at peace and pure,
join our palms and turn respectfully to you
our loving and patient Mother Earth,
as we offer words of fervent repentance. [BELL]

We have not been fortunate enough
to bring the teachings into our lives earlier,
and so we have lived in forgetfulness for a long time.
Obscured by ignorance,
we have brought about suffering
and made many foolish mistakes.
We and our ancestors
have sown our hearts' garden with unwholesome seeds.
We have been responsible for exploiting and polluting you,
our beautiful planet Earth.
Much of what we and our ancestors have done
continues to damage the environment day after day.
We repent of these countless unmindful acts
that have brought about so much unnecessary suffering.
We vow to begin anew from today. [BELL]

We see how thoughtless we have been,
as we strayed from the path of mindfulness.
Driven by craving, ignorance, and fear,
we have treated you as something other than ourselves.
Troubled by anxiety,
we have failed to protect you,
and to see that we are all your children.
Angry and resentful, we blame each other,
and polarize the world into separate factions.
Unable to speak to or look at others with eyes of compassion,
we create suffering that lasts a long time.
Now we turn to you our mother,
and in sincere repentance we bow our heads. [BELL]

We know that in the human consciousness
are buried countless wholesome seeds
of love and understanding,
and of peace and joy.
But because we have not known how to water them,
they have not sprouted fresh and green.
We have grown used to chasing a distant happiness,
which causes us to exploit your resources.
Our mind is constantly occupied by the past
or travelling far into the future.
We are caught in a cycle of craving.
Unable to appreciate the precious things we have,
we seek happiness in consumption.
This has led to the devastation of the environment,
which will last for a very long time,
causing suffering for our children and their children.
Now in this hall, fragrant with incense,
we vow to change and begin anew. [BELL]

With sincerity and respect,
we turn to you, Great Mother Earth
and all the great beings
who are courageously protecting you.
Our deep aspiration is to cherish and protect you,
and not repeat the mistakes we have made.
We vow to live in an awakened way,
to train according to the true teachings.
We vow to practice mindful breathing and smiling,
and diligently live in mindfulness. [BELL]

We will come back to ourselves
and live in the wonderful present moment,
to sow wholesome seeds in our hearts' garden,
and to cultivate understanding and love.
We will learn to look deeply
and practice deep understanding,
to see the true nature of all that is
and free ourselves from the suffering

brought about by the notion of birth and death.
We will practice right action,
and care for you and all species throughout the day,
bringing the source of joy to many places,
helping all to suffer less,
and repaying the deep gratitude we owe
to parents, teachers, friends, and all beings.
With faith we light up the incense of our heart.
We turn to you, our Compassionate Mother
and vow to protect you
by training ourselves diligently
on the wonderful path of practice.
[BELL, BELL]
[Everyone stands up]

5. TOUCHING THE EARTH

[Head of ceremony reads]
We see the virtues of stability and perseverance in you, Mother Earth,
We return to you and take refuge.
We aspire to live so that you can have confidence in us.
With one-pointed mind we touch the earth
before the refreshing and pure Bodhisattva,
our Mother Earth, always there to protect, nourish, and heal.
[BELL]
[Everyone touches the earth]

[Head of ceremony reads as the community is in the prostrate position.]
Taking refuge in the earth.
[Wake up bell, for everyone to stand up]

As a human species we have not given back to the earth as much as we have taken from it. We have exploited the earth's natural resources and polluted the environment. We touch the earth to express regret. [BELL]
[Everyone touches the earth]

Expressing regret for exploiting the earth.
[Wake up bell, for everyone to stand up]

We are putting so much strain on the earth by polluting the atmosphere, warming the planet, and poisoning the oceans, that the earth cannot heal herself any more on her own. We aspire to do all we can to help the earth heal.
[BELL]
[Everyone touches the earth]

Helping the earth heal.
[Wake up bell, for everyone to stand up]

We have lost contact with the earth's natural rhythm and that is the cause of much modern sickness. We aspire to take better care of ourselves. We cannot just rely on the earth to take care of us. We also need to take care of the earth.
[BELL]
[Everyone touches the earth]

Taking care of ourselves, taking care of the earth.
[Wake up bell, for everyone to stand up]

We realize that the conditions needed to restore earth's balance come from inside of us, from our own mindfulness and level of awareness. Our awakened consciousness is what can heal the earth.
[BELL]
[Everyone touches the earth]

Healing the earth with awareness.
[Wake up bell, for everyone to stand up]

There is a revolution that needs to happen and it starts from inside each one of us. When we realize that we and the earth are one, our own suffering will start to ease, and we will have the compassion and understanding to treat the earth with love and respect. We vow to look deeply every day to see that we and the earth are one.
[BELL]
[Everyone touches the earth]

We and the earth are one.
[Wake up bell, for everyone to stand up]

6. Intimate Conversation with the Earth While Touching the Earth

Dear Mother, there are times when we suffer greatly because of natural disasters. We know that at those times you are also suffering greatly. Sometimes we turn to you and ask: "Can we count on you?" You do not answer immediately. After a while, you look at us with the eyes of great compassion and say: "Dear children, of course you can count on me. I shall always be there for you. Though, please ask yourselves the question: can Mother Earth trust and count on you?" [BELL]
[Everyone touches the earth]

[Read while everyone touches the earth]
Dear Mother Earth, we have stayed awake many nights with this question and now with tears in our eyes we come before you and give you this answer from our hearts: "Dear compassionate and loving mother, you can count on us."
[Three breaths]

Dear mother, we know that you want us to live in a way that at every moment of our daily life we can give rise to mindfulness, peace, stability, and love.
[Three breaths]
We have an unshakeable confidence that if our human species produces these wholesome energies daily, we shall be able to help all species suffer less from war, poverty, hunger, and disease. We shall have more joy in being alive and truly enjoy your presence. We shall also be able to reduce the number of natural disasters: floods, hurricanes, earthquakes, and tsunamis. Please, mother, be at peace. You can trust us.
[Three breaths]
[BELL, BELL]
[Everyone stands up.]

7. May the Day Be Well ♪

May the day be well and the night be well.
May the midday hour bring happiness too.
In every minute and every second,
may the day and night be well.

By the blessing of the Triple Gem,
may all things be protected and safe.
May all beings born in each of the four ways
live in a land of purity.
May all in the three realms be born upon lotus thrones.
May countless wandering souls
realize the three virtuous positions of the bodhisattva path.
May all living beings, with grace and ease,
fulfill the bodhisattva stages.
The countenance of the World-Honored One, like the full moon
or like the orb of the sun, shines with the light of clarity.
A halo of wisdom spreads in every direction,
enveloping all with love and compassion,
joy and equanimity.
Namo Shakyamunaye Buddhaya
Namo Shakyamunaye Buddhaya
Namo Shakyamunaye Buddhaya
[BELL, BELL]

8. Chant Namo 'valokitesvaraya ♪

9. Closing Verse ♪

Beginning anew, practicing the way of awareness
Gives rise to benefits without limit
We vow to share the fruit with all beings,
We vow to offer tribute to parents, teachers, friends, numerous beings
Who give guidance and support along the path.
[BELL, BELL, BELL]

Meditations and contemplations

Love (Metta) Meditation

[We begin practicing this love meditation focusing on ourselves ("I"). Next, we can practice focusing on others (substituting "you)", first on someone we like, then onsomeone neutral to us, and finally on someone who has made us suffer.]

May I be peaceful, happy, and light in body and spirit.
May I be safe and free from injury.
May I be free from anger, fear, and anxiety.

May I learn to look at myself with the eyes of understanding and love.
May I recognize and touch the seeds of joy and happiness in myself.
May I learn to identify and see the sources of anger, craving, and delusion in myself.

May I know how to nourish the seeds of joy in myself every day.
May I live fresh, solid, and free.
May I be free from attachment and aversion, but not be indifferent.

May you be peaceful, happy, and light in body and spirit.
May you be safe and free from injury.
May you be free from anger, fear, and anxiety.

May you learn to look at yourself with the eyes of
understanding and love.
May you recognize and touch the seeds of joy and happiness in yourself.
May you learn to identify and see the sources of anger, craving, and delusion in yourself.

May you know how to nourish the seeds of joy in yourself every day.
May you live fresh, solid, and free.
May you be free from attachment and aversion, but not be indifferent.

FOURTEEN VERSES ON MEDITATION

1. Just as a bird has two wings,
the practice of meditation has "stopping" and "deep looking."
The two wings depend on each other.
Stopping and deep looking go together.

2. Stopping means to be still,
in order to recognize, to be in contact
to nourish, to heal,
to calm and to focus the mind.

3. Deep looking means to regard in depth
the true nature of the Five Skandhas,
so that understanding may arise
to transform all grief and pain.

4. The breath and the footstep
generate the source of mindfulness,
which enables us to recognize
and be in touch with the wonders of life.

5. By calming our body and mind,
we nourish and heal ourselves;
we can guard our six senses,
and maintain right concentration.

6. Looking deeply into reality
to see the true nature of all dharmas,
helps us to let go
of all seeking and all fears.

7. Dwelling in the present moment,
we transform habit energies,
give rise to understanding,
and free ourselves from all afflictions.

8. Impermanence is nonself.
Nonself is interdependence,

is emptiness, is conventional designation,
is the Middle Way, is interbeing.

9. Emptiness, signlessness, and aimlessness
resolve all grief and pain.
In the daily practice
we are not caught in conceptual knowledge.

10. Nirvana is not to be attained.
Immediate and gradual enlightenment are not separate.
Realization is to live free and at ease
right in this present moment.

11. The basic meditation sutras
such as the Mindfulness of Breathing
and the Four Establishments of Mindfulness,
show us step by step how to transform the body and the mind.

12. The Mahayana sutras and shastras
open more wide doors
to help us see the depth
of meditation in Source Buddhism.

13. There should be no discrimination
between the Tathagata and the Ancestor School of meditation.
The Four Noble Truths must be taught as interdependent
in order to be a foundation for transmitting the Dharma.

14. With the support of the Sangha,
it is easy to succeed in the practice,
and accomplish quickly
the great aspiration to help all beings.

THE FIVE EARTH-TOUCHINGS

[Before each touching of the earth, the practitioner first reads the words in italics, either aloud or silently. Whilst prostrating, the practitioner contemplates the text that follows. If practicing in a group, one person can read the text aloud while the others touch the earth and contemplate.]

FIRST EARTH-TOUCHING

Touching the earth, I connect with all generations of my blood ancestors.
[BELL]
[With the sound of the bell, the practitioner or the whole group touches the earth.]
I see you my father, my mother. Your blood, your flesh, and your vitality are circulating in my veins, nourishing every cell. Through you, I see each of my grandparents. Your energy, your expectations, your experience, and your wisdom have been transmitted to me from so many generations. I carry in me the life, blood, happiness, and sorrow of all my ancestors. Suffering and shortcomings have also been passed on to me, and I am practicing to transform them. I open my heart, my flesh, my bones to receive the energy of your insight and love, as well as of your experience. I see my roots in you, my father, my mother, grandfathers, and grandmothers. I know that I am just your continuation. Please support, protect, and transmit to me still more of your energy. I am aware, dear ancestors, that wherever your children or grandchildren are living, you are present. I know that you always love and support your children and grandchildren, even though you were not always able to express your love skillfully due to your own difficulties and challenges. Dear ancestors, I am aware that you have done your best to build a way of life based on gratitude, loyalty, confidence, respect, and love. As a continuation of your lineage, I touch the earth with all my heart and allow your energy to penetrate me. I turn to you, my blood ancestors, to ask for your support, protection, and strength.
[Three breaths]
[BELL]
[with the sound of the bell, the practitioner or the whole group stand up.]

SECOND EARTH-TOUCHING

Touching the earth, I connect with all generations of my spiritual ancestors.
[BELL]

[With the sound of the bell, the practitioner or the whole group touches the earth.]
I see you in me, my spiritual teachers who guide me on the path of love and understanding, who have taught me to breathe mindfully, to smile, to forgive, to live deeply in the present moment. Through you, I can be in touch with many generations and traditions of spiritual teachers, saints, and spiritual ancestors,* going back to the ones who began my spiritual tradition thousands of years ago. Your energy enters me and creates peace, joy, understanding, and love in me to this day. I know that your energy has deeply transformed the world. Without you, I would not know the way of practice that brings peace and happiness into my life and into the life of my family and society. I open my heart, my body, and my mind to receive your experience, your wisdom, and your energy of love and protection. I am your continuation. I ask you, dear spiritual ancestors, to transmit to me your infinite source of energy, peace, stability, understanding, and love. I make the vow to practice in order to transform my suffering and the suffering of the world and to transmit your energy to future generations.
[Three breaths]
[BELL]
[With the sound of the bell, the practitioner or the whole group stand up.]

THIRD EARTH-TOUCHING

Touching the earth, I connect with this land and all the land ancestors who have made it available to us.
[BELL]
[With the sound of the bell, the practitioner or the whole group touches the earth.]

I see that I am held, protected, and nourished by this land and by you who have made life easy and possible for me here by all your efforts. I am filled with gratitude toward all the generations of those who have lived on, worked, and developed this land. I am aware that thanks to you I have all I need.

I see (*here you should insert the names of those who have helped build the country in which you are practicing*) . . . you who have used your talents, your wisdom, your patience to make this country a refuge for many people coming from all over the world. Whether your names are remembered or

*Here, you can add the names of spiritual ancestors appropriate for the practitioners present.

not, you have built schools, hospitals, places for spiritual practice, roads, bridges, and so on. Wholeheartedly, you have worked for human rights and justice, building brotherhood and sisterhood. You have advanced our understanding of the world through your curiosity and scientific research and made our lives easier. I feel your harmonious presence when walking in nature, you who have lived in peace on this land and who have known how to protect the earth. Today, I also wish to live in harmony with all species, and I feel the energy of this land penetrate my body and spirit, accepting me and supporting me. I make the vow to continue to cultivate this energy and to transmit it to future generations. I am determined to practice for the transformation of violence, hate, discrimination, and ignorance, which still exist in society, so that future generations will know joy and peace. May you and this land give me protection and support.
[*Three breaths*]
[BELL]
[*With the sound of the bell, the practitioner or the whole group stand up.*]

FOURTH EARTH-TOUCHING
Touching the earth, all the energy I have received from all my ancestors I transmit to those I love.
[BELL]
[*With the sound of the bell, the practitioner or the whole group touches the earth.*]

The unlimited energy I have received, I now transfer to you, my father, my mother, and everyone I love. In the past, you have suffered and worried because of me and for my sake. I know I have been unskilful and foolish due to not being mindful enough in my daily life. I know that you who love me have also suffered from your own difficulties. You have not always been lucky enough to have an environment that enabled you to flourish.

I transmit this wonderful source of energy to you, my mother, my father, my brother (*name*), my sister (*name*), my beloved (*name*), my child (*name*), to ease your pain and transform your suffering so that you will be able to smile again and feel the joy of being alive. With my whole heart, I wish for your physical and mental well-being, that you may be at peace and happy. Your happiness is my happiness. I promise to love and care for you, and I ask all my blood and spiritual ancestors to support and protect you. I see that I am not separate from you. I am one with you whom I love.
[*Three breaths*]

[BELL]
[*With the sound of the bell, the practitioner or the whole group stand up.*]

FIFTH EARTH-TOUCHING

Touching the earth with understanding and compassion, I transmit to the one who has made me suffer the positive energy I have received from my ancestors.
[BELL]
[*With the sound of the bell, the practitioner or the whole group touches the earth.*]

I open my heart so that I can transmit to you the energy of understanding and love, you who have made me suffer or hurt me deeply. I know that you have also been through much suffering. Your heart may be overloaded with bitterness and anger. Because you have suffered, you make others suffer. I know that you have not been lucky. As a child or adolescent, you did not receive the love and care that you needed. Life and society have dealt you many hardships. You may have been wronged and abused. You have not been guided on the path of mindful living. You have accumulated many wrong perceptions about life and about me. As a result, you have made me and my dear ones suffer. I pray to my blood and spiritual ancestors to channel to you the energy of love and protection, so that your heart can receive the nectar of compassion and blossom like a flower. All I wish for is your transformation, that you can touch the joy of being alive, that you no longer hold on to the anger, resentment, and suffering in your heart and do not continue to make yourself and others suffer. I see that your suffering has been passed down from generation to generation. I do not want to hold feelings of anger and hatred toward you. I want your suffering to end. As my heart blossoms like a flower, I can let go of blame and resentment. I channel to you my energy of compassion and understanding, and I ask my ancestors to support you.
[*Three breaths*]
[BELL]
[*With the sound of the bell, the practitioner or the whole group stand up.*]

SIXTH EARTH-TOUCHING [OPTIONAL]

Touching the earth, I connect with my original spiritual tradition.
[BELL]
[*With the sound of the bell, the practitioner or the whole group touches the earth.*]

I see myself as a child, in the church, the mosque, the temple, or the synagogue, listening to a sermon or attending a ceremony. I see the priest, the imam, the rabbi, or other people from my congregation. A time may have come when I lost faith in the religion of my childhood. I was not able to communicate my difficulties and no one was able to listen or resolve them. I abandoned my childhood faith and lost contact with the spiritual ancestors of that tradition. Having looked deeply, I am aware that there are treasures within the spiritual tradition into which I was born. This tradition has contributed to the stability, joy, and inner peace of my ancestors for generations. I know I can go back to it to rediscover its essential spiritual values, which can nourish myself and my children. As I touch the earth, I reconnect with my spiritual ancestors of my former faith and allow their energy to flow freely through me. I recognize all the teachers throughout the centuries in my former faith as my spiritual ancestors. I bow before you in the present moment, the only moment that truly counts.
[*Three breaths*]
[BELL]
[*With the sound of the bell, the practitioner or the whole group stand up.*]

EXPLANATION

The Five Earth Touchings are above all a practice of reconciliation. After practicing the first two Earth Touchings, we feel the energy from our blood and spiritual families circulating in our body and mind. We already feel stronger and more confident.

During the third Earth Touching, we get in contact with the country we are living in, the sacred energy of nature, and the people who worked the land and built a nation. Many of them worked silently without leaving their names. Even though long dead, they are still present, protecting and supporting us. After this Earth Touching, we feel like a tree with many solid roots. We have more energy.

The fourth Earth Touching is directed toward our beloved ones with whom we share the sources of energy that we have just received. At the sound of the bell, when we stand up, the discrimination that we felt between ourselves and the other disappears. We and our beloved ones become one stream of life. Our peace and our happiness become theirs. If we have a lot of solidity and energy, we can transmit it to them.

During the fifth Earth Touching, we transmit our energy to those who have made us suffer. Practicing this Earth Touching for the first time, some people feel a lot of resistance. Why should we love and transmit our energy to that person who has hurt us and created so much difficulty? But regularly practicing this Earth Touching for several weeks, we come to understand how beneficial it can be.

Practicing wholeheartedly, after several months we will feel the hatred in our hearts dissolve. It is miraculous. Some practitioners have let us know that after only six months of practice, they no longer felt the need to continue with this Earth Touching. None of the hatred remained toward the person who had made them suffer.

This is the authentic practice of compassion. The Buddha taught: do not answer hate with hate; the only response to hate is love and forgiveness. As long as we hold on to our hatred, we will continue to suffer. When we can put this teaching into practice, compassion fills our hearts. When we can forgive the other, we are healed. We will feel more at peace and at ease, touching well-being and happiness.

If we have suffered a lot and our wounds are very deep, we should practice the fifth Earth Touching every evening. To succeed, we must first succeed with the first two Earth Touchings. We need to get sufficiently in contact with our blood and spiritual ancestors to be able to receive their energy of love. At Plum Village, we practice Touching the Earth together or individually in the meditation hall. Once we have become familiar with this practice and mastered it, we can adapt the text so that it is more appropriate to our own situation.

If you were brought up in a tradition other than Buddhism, a tradition that you have now abandoned, the sixth Earth Touching can help you return to and reconcile with your roots. To be in connection with your spiritual roots is very important for your solidity and healing. With two spiritual families ("double belonging"), you will be able to enrich your spiritual life with treasures from both roots, bringing you even more joy and love.

The Three Earth-Touchings

[Before touching the earth, the practitioner reads the words in italics below, either aloud or silently. while prostrating, the practitioner contemplates the text that follows. If practicing in a group, one person can read the text aloud while the others touch the earth and contemplate.]

First Earth-Touching

Touching the earth, I connect with my ancestors and descendants, from both my spiritual and blood families.
[BELL]
[With the sound of the bell, the practitioner or the whole group touches the earth.]

My spiritual ancestors are noble teachers, saints, and realized beings throughout the ages, and also my teachers of this lifetime. Whether you are still living or you lived long ago, you are all truly present in me. You have transmitted to me the seeds of peace, wisdom, love, and happiness. You have awakened in me seeds of peace, insight, compassion, and happiness.

When I look at you, my spiritual ancestors, I see those who are perfect in the practice of the mindfulness trainings, understanding, and compassion, and those who are still imperfect. I bow down and accept you all as my spiritual ancestors, knowing that within myself are shortcomings and weaknesses.
[Three breaths]

Aware that my practice of the mindfulness trainings is not always perfect, and that I am not always as understanding and compassionate as I would like to be, I open my heart to my spiritual descendants and accept you all. Some of you practice the mindfulness trainings, understanding, and compassion in a way that invites confidence and respect. There are also those of you who are struggling with many difficulties and are constantly going through ups and downs in your practice. Aware of my own weaknesses and faults, I open my heart and accept you all.
[Three breaths]

In the same way, I accept all of you, my ancestors, on my father's side and my mother's side of the family, with all your good qualities, your talents, and your virtuous actions, as well as your faults and your weaknesses.
[Three breaths]

You, my spiritual and blood ancestors and descendants, are all present

in me. I am you and you are me. I do not have a separate self. We are all part of a wonderful stream of life constantly flowing together.
[*Three breaths*]
[BELL]
[*With the sound of the bell, the practitioner or the whole group stand up.*]

SECOND EARTH-TOUCHING

Touching the earth, I connect with all people and all species that are alive in this moment in the world with me.
[BELL]
[*With the sound of the bell, the practitioner or the whole group touches the earth.*]

I am one with the wonderful pattern of life that radiates out in all directions. I see the close connection between myself and all people and all species, how we share happiness and suffering.

I am one with the great beings who have transcended birth and death. I see how we can look at all phenomena such as birth and death, happiness and suffering, with a calm gaze. I am one with those wise spiritual friends—who can be found a little bit everywhere—who radiate peace, understanding, and love, who can touch the nourishing and healing wonders of life, who can embrace the whole world with a loving heart and arms of caring action. I am one with those who have enough peace, happiness, and freedom to be able to offer non-fear and the joy of being alive to everyone around them. I do not feel alone or cut off from others. I feel supported by the compassion and joy of great beings, who help me not to drown in despair but to live my life fully, with meaning, peace, and joy. I see myself in each one of you and I see you all in me.
[*Three breaths*]

I am one with someone who was born disabled or who has become disabled because of war, accident, or illness. I am one with someone who is caught in a situation of war, oppression, or imprisonment. I am one with someone who has never enjoyed happiness and peace in family life. Cut off from my roots, I am hungry for understanding and love, and am always looking for beauty, truth, and goodness, which can give meaning to my life and in which I can take refuge.
[*Three breaths*]

I am one with someone who is at the point of death, and I am very afraid because I do not know what will become of me. I am one with a child living in a place where there is miserable poverty and disease; my arms and legs are as thin as matchsticks, and I have no future. I am also one with a manufacturer of armaments that are sold to poor countries. I am one with the frog swimming in the pond, but I am also one with the grass snake who needs to feed on the frog. I am the caterpillar and the ant, and also the bird hunting for insects to eat. I am the forest that is being cut down, the rivers and the air that are being polluted. I am also the person who clear-cuts the forest and pollutes the river and the air. I see myself in all species, and I see all species in me.

[*Three breaths*]

[BELL]

[*Then with the sound of the bell, the practitioner or the whole group stand up.*]

THIRD EARTH-TOUCHING

Touching the earth, I let go of all ideas that I am this body and this limited life span.

[BELL]

[*With the sound of the bell, the practitioner or the whole group touches the earth.*]

I know that this body, made of the four elements (earth, water, air, fire), is not truly me, I am not limited by this body. I am a river of the life of spiritual and blood ancestors, which since beginningless time has flowed to the present and will continue to stream onward into the future without end. I am both my ancestors and my descendants. I am life manifesting in thousands of forms. I inter-am with all people and all species, whether they are peaceful and fearless or suffering and afraid. In this moment, I am present everywhere on this planet. I am also present in the past and in the future. The disintegration of this body does not touch me, just as the falling plum blossoms do not mean the end of the plum tree. I see myself as a wave on the surface of the ocean. My true nature is the ocean water. I see myself in all the other waves, and I see all the other waves in me. The appearance or disappearance of the form of the wave does not affect the ocean.

My Dharma body and spiritual life are not subject to birth and death. I see myself present before the manifestation of this body and after its decomposition. Even in this moment, I see how I exist elsewhere than in this body. My life span is not limited to eighty or ninety years. My life span, just like the life span of a leaf or the buddhas, is unlimited. I can go beyond the idea that I am a body separate in space and time from all other manifestations of life.

[*Three breaths*]

[BELL]

[*With the sound of the bell, the practitioner or the whole group stand up.*]

EXPLANATION

We suffer because we are caught by the notions of me, the other, and life span. The Three Earth Touchings help us to transcend all these notions. Practicing the first Earth Touching, we visualize our ancestors and our descendants. We prostrate ourselves, with our four limbs and forehead touching the ground. The closer our body can be in contact with the earth, the better. In this position, we start to relax all the muscles of our body. We let go of everything we consider to be "me" or "mine" so that we can become one with the stream of life of our ancestors and descendants, which is our own stream of life. We have both blood and spiritual ancestors and descendants.

When we touch the earth like this, we can more easily reconcile with our ancestors. If we are angry with our father, our mother, our teacher, our brother, or our sister, this Earth Touching will help us to reconcile with them. Our father, mother, uncles, aunts, brothers, and sisters are all our ancestors and descendants. Each one born before us is our ancestor. Each one born after us is our descendant. Some of our ancestors had many talents, and some were unskilful. Nevertheless, they are our ancestors, and we have to accept them all. Our ancestors, descendants, parents, our brothers and sisters, all have certain good qualities as well as some shortcomings. The same is true for ourselves. Therefore we accept them as they are. Whether they are skilful or unskilful, they are still our ancestors and descendants. Our parents are simply parents. Whether they were good or unsatisfactory parents, they are still our parents.

Our teachers have given birth to our spiritual life, and have accepted us as their students. In the same way we accept our fellow practitioners and our teachers. Even if they have shortcomings, their ups and downs, and they make mistakes, they are still our spiritual ancestors and descendants. Our acceptance and reconciliation is the only path that can help them. It is important to practice the first Earth Touching every day, with all our heart, especially when we have difficulties with our our teachers, and fellow practitioners.

During the second Earth Touching, we are in touch with all people and all beings alive in the present moment. As in the first exercise, we contemplate the text while prostrating with our four limbs and forehead on the earth. We can turn to the bodhisattvas, great beings alive in the world in this moment. Whether we call them "bodhisattvas" or not, they are bodhisattvas because they have solidity, freedom, and love. They are a little bit everywhere, for example, in humanitarian organizations like Doctors Without Borders or Schools Without Borders. There are so many people everywhere in the world working to relieve suffering thanks to their love, solidity, and freedom. Amongst those engaged in humanitarian work, some have solidity, freedom, peace, and happiness. Thanks to these qualities, they do not drown in the ocean of suffering that they face daily.

We can connect with them, take refuge in them, to become stronger. They are very close; in fact, right here. They are not necessarily elders. Sometimes they are still very young, but we can already recognize in them the solidity, freedom, peace, and happiness that we need. We feel gratitude for their presence. Now that we have touched the energy of bodhisattvas, we can get in contact with beings who are still drowning in the ocean of suffering: the victims of wars in the Middle East, hungry children in the developing world, prisoners, people who are suffering, oppressed and exploited, children who did not have the chance to go to school and instead have to search for scraps of food thrown out with the rubbish . . . They are all us. We are the frog who swims freely in the autumn pond, but the snake needs food to survive as well. This kind of suffering is part of life. When we are in touch with the suffering of all beings, we do not drown in it, because we have a place of refuge. The bodhisattvas and great beings are our refuge. They are present in our sangha. Those who suffer are also in our sangha. We are one with them. As soon as we recognize this, our facial expression as we look at them will already communicate that we understand their suffering.

The third Earth Touching encompasses time and space. "Touching the earth, I abandon the idea that I am only this body." In France, a group of women have been protesting for their right to choose abortion. Concurrently, another group of women organized a protest march against the first group. Those who support the right to choose defend their view in this way: this body is mine; I must have the right to do what I like with my body. According to Buddhist wisdom, this view is not quite right: our body is not only ours; it also belongs to our ancestors, our parents, our descendants, to humanity and the whole cosmos. The peace and joy of my body are linked to the peace and joy of other bodies.

In the third Earth Touching, we see that we are not only this body, which was born on a certain day of a certain month in a certain year. The Buddha has reminded us of this truth in numerous sutras: this body is not me. When we practice correctly the first Earth Touching, we can already see this truth: our ancestors are us; our parents, our brothers, our sisters, and our children are us. We are so much more than we think we are. In this Earth Touching, we unite ourselves with the whole stream of life. What I consider to be "me" transcends the limits of this physical body.

I train myself to abandon the belief that this body is me, and that I am only this body. I practice to understand that my life span is not limited to eighty or ninety years. I can see my existence before the manifestation of this body and after its decomposition. My life span is unlimited. This is the third Touching of the Earth. The insight from the third exercise comes from practicing the first and second. If we have succeeded in practicing the first two, we have already practiced the third.

Practicing deeply these Earth Touchings every day, we can liberate ourselves from birth and death.

The Five Remembrances

[*These five remembrances help us to identify and look deeply at the seeds of fear. They can be recited daily, read aloud as a guided meditation, or used as a silent meditation by individual practitioners.*]

I am of the nature to grow old.
There is no way to escape growing old.
[BELL]

I am of the nature to have ill-health.
There is no way to escape having ill-health.
[BELL]

I am of the nature to die.
There is no way to escape death.
[BELL]

All that is dear to me and everyone I love are of the nature to change.
There is no way to escape being separated from them.
[BELL]

I inherit the results of my actions of body, speech, and mind.
The results of my actions are the only thing I can take with me into the future.
[BELL, BELL]

The Five Awarenesses

[*These verses are used in the wedding ceremony, see page 123. They are also to be recited by couples on the full-moon and new-moon days.*]

We are aware that all generations of our ancestors
and all future generations are present in us.
[BELL]

We are aware of the expectations that our ancestors, our children,
and their children have of us.
[BELL]

We are aware that our joy, peace, freedom, and harmony
are the joy, peace, freedom, and harmony
of our ancestors, our children, and their children.
[BELL]

We are aware that understanding is the very foundation of love.
[BELL]

We are aware that blaming and arguing can never help us
and only create a wider gap between us;
that only understanding, trust, and love can help us change and grow.
[BELL, BELL]

CONTEMPLATION TO BE READ BEFORE A SANGHA MEETING

Dear Lord Buddha and teachers over many generations,

We vow to go through this meeting in a spirit of togetherness as we review all ideas and consolidate them to a harmonious understanding (consensus). We vow to use loving speech and deep listening in order to bring about the success of this meeting, as an offering to the Three Jewels. We vow not to hesitate to share our ideas and insights but also vow not to say anything when the feeling of irritation is present in us. We are determined not to allow tension to build up in this meeting. If any one of us recognizes tension, we will ask for the bell to be invited. Those who feel responsible for contributing to the tension may then apologize, so that the atmosphere of togetherness and harmony can be restored.

[BELL]

CONTEMPLATION BEFORE A SHINING LIGHT SESSION

When I look at you, I see you as a flowing stream and not a separate self to reproach or to praise. Looking into you, I see your ancestors, your lineage, your parents, your homeland, your culture, the things that are great and beautiful, and the things that are not yet great and beautiful.

You are a wonderful manifestation, a flower in the garden of humanity. I am aware of your presence and I cherish your presence. I also hope that you see me as a flowing stream, and not a separate self to reproach, to criticize, or to praise. We are brothers and sisters of each other in this Sangha. Therefore, I have you in me and you have me in you. We must support and encourage each other to cultivate further the things that are great and beautiful in us, and to transform those things that are not yet so great and beautiful. If I say something to help you transform, it is not a reproach but it is my hope for you. Looking into me, you also see the things that are unskilful and imperfect, and if you were to say something to me, it would not be a criticism or a reproach, but only a hope for me to transform. When you transform, I can be happier, and when I transform, you can be happier. We support one another on the path of practice. We need each other. I deeply cherish your presence in our community.

NOTE ON THE PRACTICE OF SHINING LIGHT

Shining light was once a practice reserved for monks and nuns. In the Plum Village tradition it is also practiced by lay order members. The practice is to help one another see ourselves more clearly in terms of our positive and negative qualities; what we have already achieved and what we need to practice more.

It is a deep practice of understanding and love. It should only be practiced by those who have known each other for at least a year.

music

MORNING CHANT

The Dhar ma bo -

- dy___ is shi ning bright ly - - as the day

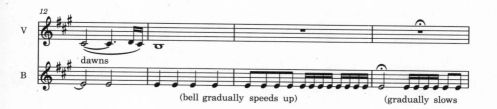

dawns   (bell gradually speeds up)   (gradually slows

In stillness   we   sit   our hearts are...

down)

2

EVENING CHANT: VERSION 1

Very slowly, with bell   Adapted from a traditional Vietnamese chant

Sta - bly___ sea - ted u - - - n - der the___

Bo - - - - - dhi___ tree.___ Bo - dy, speech, and

mi - - nd a - re one in sti - ll - ness,___

free_____ from vie - ws of ri - ght a - nd wro - ng.

When we are fo - cused in per - fect mind - fu - l - ness, our true nature

is i - llu - mi - ned. The sho - - - re of con -

fu - sion is le - - - - - ft be - hi - nd.

No - ble San - gha, di - li - gent - ly bring your mind in - to me - di - ta - tion.

Call and response three times

Na - mo___ Sha - kya - mu - na - ye Bu - ddha - ya

Evening Chant: version 2

Very slowly, with bell

Music by Chan Phap Hien

With po-sture u-pright and sta - ble,

we are sea - ted at the foot of the Bo - dhi tree.___

___ Bo - dy, speech, and mi - nd a - re

o - ne i - n still - ness; there is no more thought

of ri - ght and wro - ng. Our mind and bo-dy dwell

in pe - r-fect mind-ful - ness. We re - di - sco - ver our o - ri - gi-nal na -

ture, lea - ving the shore of i - llu - sion be - hi - nd.

No-ble Sang-ha, di-li-gent - ly bring your mind in-to me-di-ta - tion.

Call and response 3 times

Na - mo___ Sha - kya-mu-na - ye Bu - ddha - ya

LISTENING TO THE BELL

Text by Thích Nhất Hạnh

Music by Chan Phap Linh

2

INCENSE OFFERING

Slowly

Music by Chan Phap Hien

In gra - ti - tude, we o - ffer this in - cense through-out space and time to all Bu - ddhas and Bo - dhi - satt - vas. May it be fra - grant as Earth her - self, re - flec - ting care - ful e - fforts, whole - hear - ted a - ware - ness, and the fruit of un - der - stan - ding slow - ly ri - pe - ning. Ma - y we and all be - ings be com - pa - nions of Bu - ddhas and Bo - dhi - satt - vas. Ma - y we a - wa - ken from for - get - ful - ness and rea - lize our true ho - me.

INTRODUCTORY VERSE

Chanted flowingly

Music by Dana Maiban

Solo:
The one who bows and the one who is bowed to

Chorus:
a - re both, by na - tu - re, e - mp - ty.

There - fore the co-mmu-ni - ca - tion be - twee - n them

is i - nex - pre - ssi - bly per - fect.

Our prac - tice cen - ter is the Net of In - dra

re - flec - ting all Bu-ddhas e - v'ry - where.

And with my per - son in front of each Bu - ddha,

I go with my whole life for re - fuge.

TOUCHING THE EARTH

Chanted flowingly   Adapted from music by Dana Maiban

O - ffe -ring light   in the Ten   Di - rec - tions,

the Bu - ddha,   the Dhar - ma,   and the Sa - ng - ha

to whom we bow   in   gra - ti - tude._____

Tea - ching and li - ving the way of a - ware - ness

in the ve - ry midst of   su - ffe -ring and con - fu - sion,

Sha - kya mu - ni Bu - ddha,   the   Fu - lly En -ligh -tened One,

to whom we bow   in   gra - ti - tude._____

Verses:

Cutting through ignorance,
awakening our hearts and our
minds,
Manjushri, the Bodhisattva of
Great Understanding,
to whom we bow in gratitude.

Working mindfully, working
joyfully for the sake of all beings,
Samantabhadra, the Bodhisattva
of Great Action,
to whom we bow in gratitude.

Listening deeply, serving beings
in countless ways,
Avalokiteshvara, the Bodhisattva
of Great Compassion,
to whom we bow in gratitude.

Fearless and persevering through
realms of suffering and darkness,
Kshitigarbha, the Bodhisattva of
Great Aspiration,
to whom we bow in gratitude.

Mother of buddhas, bodhisattvas,
and all beings, nourishing,
holding, and healing all,
Bodhisattva Gaia, Great Mother
Earth, precious jewel of the
cosmos, to whom we bow in
gratitude.
[BELL}

Radiating light in all directions,
source of life on earth,
Mahavairocana Tathagata, Great
Father Sun, Buddha of Infinite
Light and Life, to whom we bow
in gratitude.
[BELL}

Seed of awakening and loving
kindness in children and all
beings,
Maitreya, the Buddha to-be-born,
to whom we bow in gratitude.

[CONTINUE WITH THE FOLLOWING
OPTIONAL VERSES, OR SKIP TO THE
FINAL VERSE BELOW]

Seeing the Buddha in everyone,
Sadaparibhuta, the Bodhisattva of
Constant Respect,
to whom we bow in gratitude.

Convener of the Sangha, the
teacher Mahakashyapa,
to whom we bow in gratitude.

Wise elder brother, the teacher
Shariputra,
to whom we bow in gratitude.

Showing love for parents, the
teacher Mahamaudgalyayana,
to whom we bow in gratitude.

Master of the Vinaya, the teacher
Upali,
to whom we bow in gratitude.

Recorder of the teachings, the
teacher Ananda,
to whom we bow in gratitude.

The first bhikshuni, Mahagotami,
to whom we bow in gratitude.

Showing the way fearlessly and
compassionately,
the stream of all our ancestral
teachers,
to whom we bow in gratitude.

OPENING VERSE

The Sutra of the Insight That Brings Us to the Other Shore

Music by Chan Phap Linh

2

tain-ment are al-so not se-pa-rate self en-ti-ties. Who e-ver can see this no lon-ger needs

a - ny-thing to at - tain. Bo-dhi - sat-tvas who prac-tice the In-sight that Brings Us to the

O-ther Shore see no more ob-sta-cles in their mind, and be cause there are no more ob-sta-cles in thei

mind, they can o-ver-come all fear, de - stroy all wrong per - cep-tions and re-a - lise Per - fect Nir-

va - na. "All Bud-dhas in the past, pre-sent and fu-ture by prac-ti-cing the In-sight that

Brings Us to the O - ther Shore are all ca-pa-ble of at- tain-ing Au- then-tic and Per - fect En

ligh-ten- ment. "There-fore Sa-ri- pu - tra it should be known that the In - sight that

Brings Us to the O - ther Shore is a Great Man-tra, the most il - lu-mi-na-ting man-tra, the high-es

man-tra, a man-tra be yound com pare, the True Wis-dom that has the po-wer to put an

end to all kinds of suf-fer-ing. There-fore let us pro - claim a

man-tra to praise the In - sight that Brings Us to the O - ther Shore:

Ga - te, Ga - te, Pa - ra - ga - te, Pa - ra-sam- ga - te, Bo - dhi Sva-ha!

The Four Gratitudes

Chanted flowingly

Music by Chan The Nghiem

In gra-ti-tude to our fa-ther and mo-ther who have gi-ven us life,

we bow dee-ply be-fore the Three Je-wels in the Te - n Dir-rec-tions.

In gra-ti-tude to our tea-chers who have shown us the way to love,

un - der-stand, and live dee - ply the pre - sent mo - ment,

we bow dee-ply be-fore the Three Je-wels in the Te - n Dir-rec-tions.

In gra - ti - tude to our friends who guide us and

su - pport us in di - ffi - cult mo - ments,

we bow dee-ply be-fore the Three Je-wels in the Te - n Dir-rec-tions.

In gra-ti-tude to all be-ings in the a-ni-mal, plant, and mi-ne-ral worlds,

we bow dee-ply be-fore the Three Je-wels in the Te - n Dir-rec-tions.

SHARING THE MERIT

Slowly   Traditional

Re - ci - ting the su - tras, prac - ti - cing the wa - y of a -

wa - re - ness gives rise to be - ne - fits wi - thout li - mit.

We vow to share the fruits with all be - ings.

We vow to o - ffer tri - bute to pa - rents, tea - chers,

friends, and nu - me - rous be - ings who give

gui - dance and su - pport a - long the path.

MAY THE DAY BE WELL

Chanted breath by breath

Music by Chan Phap Hien

May the day be well and the night be well.

May the mid - day hour bring ha - ppi - ness too.

In e - ve - ry mi - nute and e - ve - ry se - cond,

may the day and night be well. By the ble - ssing

of the Tri - ple Gem, may all things be pro - tec - ted and safe.

May all be - ings bo - rn in each of the four ways

live in a la - nd of pu____ ri - ty.

WE ARE TRULY PRESENT

Chanted breath by breath   Music by Chan Phap Hien

With hearts e-sta-blished in mind-ful-ness,   we are tru-ly pre-sent

for si-tting and wal-king me-di-ta-tion,   and for re-ci-ting the su-tras.

May this prac-tice cen-ter, with its Four-fold San-gha,

be su-ppor-ted by the Three Je-wels and Ho-ly Be-ings,

well pro-tec-ted from the eight mis-for-tunes and the three paths of su-ffe-ring.

May pa-rents, tea-chers, friends, and all be-ings wi-thin the three realms

be filled with the most di-vine grace, and may it be found that in the world

In the world the A-wa-kened One re-lieves bi-tter-ness and su-ffe-ring.

In e-v'ry place the A-wa-kened Mind re-veals love and com-pa-ssion.

Na - mo_____ Sha - kya - -

mu - na - - - ye_____ Bu - ddha - ya.

mu - na - ye_____ Bu - ddha - ya.

From the Depths of Understanding

With drum and bell

Music by Chan Phap Hien

From the de - pths of un - der - sta - n - ding,

a flow - er o - f great e - loquence blooms:___ The

Bo - dhi - satt - va sta - nds ma - jes - ti - cally___ u - pon the

wa - ves of birth and dea - th, free__ from a - ll a - ffli - c - tions.

Her great com - pa - ssion e - li - mi - nates a - ll

si - ckness, e - ven that once thought of as in - cu - ra - ble.

Her won - drous light swee - ps a - wa - y all

ob - sta - cles and da - n - gers. The wi - llow branch, once

wa - ved re - vea - ls count - less Bu - ddha lands. Her

lo- tus flo - wer blo - ssoms a mul - ti-tude of prac - tice cen - ters. We bo - w to her. We see___ her true pre - sence in the here and now. We o - ffer her the i - n-cense of our hearts. May the Bo - dhi-satt - va ___ of Deep Li - ste - ning___ em - bra - ce us all with Great Com - pa - ssion.___ Na - mo - 'va - lo - ki - tesh-va-ra ya ___ Na - mo - 'va - lo - ki - tesh-va-ra - ya___ Na - mo - 'va - lo - ki - -tesh - va - ra - - - - ya___

THE FOUR RECOLLECTIONS

Chanted breath by breath   Music by Chan Phap Hien

The No - ble Tea - cher in whom I take re - fuge

is the One who em - bo-dies and re-veals the Ul - ti-mate Re - a - li - ty,

is the One who is wor - thy of all re - spect and o - ffe -rings,

is the One who is en - dowed with per - fec - ted wis - dom,·

is the One who is en - dowed with right un - der - stan - ding

and com - pa - ssio - nate ac - tion,

is the One who ha - ppi - ly crossed to the shore of free - dom,

is the One who looked dee - ply to know the wo - rld well,

is the high - est char - i - o - tee - r trai - ning hu - man - kind,

is the Co‑mmu‑ni‑ty that goes in the di‑rec‑tion of good‑ness,

in the di‑rec‑tion of truth, in the di‑rec‑tion of beau‑ty,

in the di‑rec‑tion of right‑teous‑ness; is the Co‑mmu‑ni‑ty that is com‑posed

of four pairs and eight kinds of ho‑ly peo‑ple;

is the Co‑mmu‑ni‑ty that is wo‑r‑thy of o‑ffe‑rings,

wo‑r‑thy of great re‑spect, wo‑r‑thy of ad‑mi‑ra‑tion,

wo‑r‑thy of sa‑lu‑ta‑tion; is the Co‑mmu‑ni‑ty

stan‑ding u‑po‑n the high‑est field of me‑rit in a‑ll of the world.

The Mind‑ful‑ness Trai‑nings,

the whole‑some way of li‑ving taught by my No‑ble Tea‑cher

is the won‑der‑ful prac‑tice that re‑mains un‑bro‑ken,

that re-mains har-mo-ni-ous,   that re-mains flaw-less, that re-mains re-fined;

is   the won-der-ful prac - tice   that   has   the   ca-pa - ci - ty

to   pre-vent wrong - do - ing   and   to   pre-vent   dan - ger;

is   the won-der-ful prac - tice   that   has   the   ca-pa - ci - ty

to   pro-tect   self   and   o - thers   and   to   re - veal   beau - ty;

is   the won-der-ful prac - tice   that is   lea-ding to con-cen-tra - tion,

lea-ding to peace-ful - ness,   lea-ding to in - sight,   lea-ding to   non-fear;

is   the won-der-ful prac - tice   that   shows   us   the   wa - y

rit.

to   to - tal e-man - ci-pa - tion   and long - la - sting ha - ppi - ness.

INVOCATION OF THE BUDDHA AND BODHISATTVAS

Moderately, with drum and bell

Music from *Om Namo Bhagavate*, by Praful

Om Na-mo_____ Sa-ma - n-ta - bha - dra -

ya Bo - dhi-sa - ttva - - ya_____

Om Na-mo_____ 'va-lo - ki - te-shva - ra -

ya Bo - dhi-sa - ttva - - ya_____

Namo'valokiteshvaraya

Joyfully Sharing the Merit

Ble-ssed Ones who dwe - ll in the wo-rld, grant to us com-

pa - ssion. In this, and count-less li - ves be-fo -

re, fro-m be - gi-nning-less ti - - me, our mis -

takes have caused much su-ffe-ring to our-selves and o -

thers. We have done wro-ng, en-cou-raged o-thers to

do wrong, and gi - ven our con-se-nt to acts of ki-lling,

stea-ling, de-cei - ving, se-xual mis-con-duct, and o-ther

harm-ful ac-tions a - mong the Ten Un-whole-some Deeds.

Whe-ther our faults are kno - wn to o - thers or

before, we have gi - ven, even if on - ly a hand - ful

of food or sim-ple gar-ment; if we have e - ver spo-ken kind-ly,—

— e - ven if on - ly a few words; if we have e - ver

looked with eyes of com - pa - ssion, e-ven if on-ly for a mo-

ment; if we have e - ver com - for-ted—— or con-soled,

e - ven if on - ly once or twice; if we have e - ver

lis-tened care - fu-lly to won-der-ful teach-ings,—— e-ven if on-ly to

one talk; if we have e - ver o - ffered a meal to

monks a - nd nuns, e - ven if on - ly once;—— if we have e-

— ver sa-ved a life,—— e-ven if on-ly that of an ant or a worm;—

126 fruit of the high - est path. O - pe - ning our hearts

130 wide to the Per-fect High-est A - wa - ke-ning, we are re -

134 solved to a - ttain Great Un-der - stan-ding. We___ will

137 rea - lize___ com - pa - ssion and em - bo - dy deep love.

140 We___ will prac - tice di - li - gent - ly, trans -

143 for-ming our su - ffe-ring and the su-ffe-ring of all o-ther spe-cies.

146 Please trans - fer the me - rits___ of bo - dy,

149 speech, and mind to the ha - ppi-ness of peo - ple and

153 all o - ther be-ings. A - part from bo-dhi - ci - tta and a-

156 part from the thirst for great un-der-stan-ding, and the em-bo-diment

of love, there is no o-ther de-si - re wi-thin us.___

163 All Bu-ddhas in the Three Times and the Te-n Di-rec-tions___

166 ___ have o-ffered their me-rit as we are do-ing to-

169 day. Re-pen-ting all our faults,___ we joy-fu-lly con-tri-

171 bute to the i-mmea-sura-ble o-cean of me-rit

174 and the to-we-ring peaks of the high-est un-der-stan-ding.

176 The Bu-ddhas and the An-ces-tral Tea-chers

178 are the light which shows us the way.

180 In this so-lemn mo-ment,___ with all my life's

force, I come back to my-self and bow dee-ply with re-spect.

THE REFUGE CHANT

ding and com - pa - ssion wi - ll flo - wer,___ hel - ping li - ving be -

ings   be   free___   from   their   su - ffe - ring.

May the Bu-ddha, the Dhar-ma, and the Sang-ha su - pport my e - ffo-rts.

THE THREE REFUGES

Chanted breath by breath

Music by Chan Phap Hien

I take re - fuge in the Bu - ddha,

the one who shows me the wa - y in this life.

I take re - fuge in the Dha - r - ma,

the way of un - der - stan - ding and of love.

I take re - fuge in the Sa - ng - ha, the co - mmu - ni - ty that lives

in har - mo - ny and a - ware - ness. Dwe - lling in the re - fuge of Bu - ddha,

I clear - ly see the path of light and beau - ty in the world.

Dwe - lling in the re - fuge of Dhar - ma,

I learn to o - pen ma - ny doors on the path of trans - for - ma - tion.

Dwelling in the refuge of Sangha, shining light that supports me,

keeping my practice free of obstruction.

Taking refuge in the Buddha in myself,

I aspire to help all people recognize their own awakened nature,

realizing the Mind of Love. Taking refuge in the Dharma in myself,

I aspire to help all people fully master the ways of practice

and walk together on the path of liberation.

Taking refuge in the Sangha in myself,

I aspire to help all people build Four-fold Communities,

to embrace all beings and support their transformation.

PRAISING THE THREE JEWELS

Text by Thích Nhất Hạnh

Music by Chan Phap Linh

1. The Bud - dha__ jewel shines in - fi - nite - ly, en - light-ened for count- less__ life - times. The
2. The Dhar- ma__ jewel is in-fi-nite-ly lovely, the pre - cious words of __ Bud - dha. Like
3. The San- gha__ jewel is in-fi-nite-ly pre-cious, a field_ of me-rit and good seeds.__ The

beau - ty and sta - bi - li - ty of Bud - dha__ sit - ting is seen in moun-tains and
Fra - grant flo - wers__ floa - ting__ down_____ from_____ the__
three_____ robes_ and__ beg - ging bowl_ are sym - bols of_

ri - vers. How_ splen - did is the__ vul - ture__ peak how beau - ti - ful the
hea - vens. The__ won - der - ful_____ Dhar - ma is plain__ to_
free - dom. The__ mind - ful - ness_____ train - ings____ con - cen - tra - tion and

light,_____ that_ shines forth from_ Bud - dha's_ brow il - lu - mi-ning the six dark
see,__ it is re - cor - ded_____ lu - mi - nous-ly in three_____ trans - pa - rent
in - sight__ sup - port_____ each_ o - ther. In mind - ful-nes day and

paths. To the Na - ga - push - pa as - sem - bly we_____ will
bas - kets. From_ ge - ne - ra - tion to ge - ne - ra-tion han-ded down in ten di -
night, the_ San - gha dwells and_ is the foun da-tion for us to re - a -

go,__ to con - ti - nue the true_____ teac - chings and prac - ti -
rec-tions, so that to - day_____ we can see our_ way. We vow to learn with all our
lize__ the_ fruit_____ of_ me - di ta-tion. With one_____ heart we come

ces.__ We take re - fuge in the Bud-dha e - ver pre-sent.
heart._____ We take re - fuge in the Dhar-ma e - ver pre-sent.
home_____ and take re - fuge in the San-gha e - ver pre-sent.

PRAISING THE BUDDHA

Text by Thích Nhất Hạnh

Music by Chan Phap Linh

voice

The Bud - dha is like the fresh full moon that soars a-cross the im mense sky, when the

ri - ver of mind is tru - ly calm the deep wa - ters per - fect-ly mir-ror the ra - di-ance of the

moon. The coun - te-nance of the world ho-noured one like the full moon or the orb of the sun, shines

forth bright wis - dom's ha- - lo, em bra cing all with love, com-pas - sion, joy and in-clu-sive ness. May the

Way of the Bud-dha grow e-ver more bright and all beings re ceive the Dhar-ma rain, May com-pas-sion cool the

flames of the world, and wis-dom shine through the clouds of con-fu-sion re - vea-ling to all the

path. May Mo-ther Earth be pro-tec-ted and safe, May the peo-ple in the world be e-qual and free, May the

winds and the rains be in har-mo - ny, May the land be at peace in all di-rec - tions and the peo-ple em-brace the

path. May the Sangha prac-tice di-li gent-ly, sho-wing love and con-cern for one and all, just as for our ve-ry own

fa - mi-ly, trans-for - ming our hearts and minds we as pire to fol - low all great beings. With

one heart we vow to prac-tice the way of all Bo-dhi - sat - tvas, of Sa - man - ta-

-bha - dra and A - va-lo - ki-tesh - va-ra the way of per-fec - ted wis - - dom.

THE FIVE REMEMBRANCES

Music by Joseph Emet

INVOKING AVALOKITESHVARA

Adapted from the original text
Music by Chan The Nghiem

We in - voke you - r name, A - va - lo - ki - tesh -
va - ra._____ We a - spire to learn your wa - y o - f li - ste - ning in
or - der to help re - lieve the su - ff'ring in the world. You know how to
li - sten in or - der to un - de - r - sta - nd.
Na - mo 'va - lo - ki - tesh - va - ra - ya_____ Mm We invoke you - r name in or - der to prac - tice li - ste - ning with
all our a - tte - n - tion and o - pen - hear - ted-ness.
We will sit and li - sten wi - thout pre - ju - dice.

THE SONG OF NO-COMING AND NO-GOING

Adapted from a poem by Thich Nhat Hanh
Music by Rashani

THE THREE REFUGES SONG

Quickly

Music by Betsy Rose

I take re - fuge___ in the Budd - ha,____ the one who
I take re - fuge___ in the Dhar - ma,____ the way of
I take re - fuge___ in the Sang - ha, the co - mmu - ni -

shows me___ the wa - y in this life. Na - mo Budd - ha - ya, Na - mo
un - de - r - sta - n - ding and love. Na - mo Dhar - ma - ya, Na - mo
ty____ o - f mind - ful har - mo - ny. Na - mo Sang - ha - ya, Na - mo

Budd - ha - ya, Na - mo Bu - dd - ha - ya.
Dhar - ma - ya, Na - mo Dha - r - ma - ya.
Sang - ha - ya, Na - mo Sa - ng - ha - ya.

THE TWO PROMISES

Music by Betsy Rose

I____ vow to de-ve-lop un-der-sta-n-ding in
I____ vow to de-ve-lop my com-pa - ssion in

or - der to live peace-fu - lly with peo-ple, a-ni-mals, plants, and
or - der to pro - tect the lives of peo-ple, a-ni-mals, plants, and

mi-ne-rals, a - ni-mals, plants, and mi-ne-rals. Mmm ahh, mmm
mi-ne-rals, a - ni-mals, plants, and mi-ne-rals. Mmm ahh, mmm

ahh, mmm ahh.
ahh, mmm ahh.

WATERING SEEDS OF JOY

Adapted from the original text
Music by Chan The Nghiem

My mo - ther,____ my fa - ther, they a - re i - n me,

and when I look, I see my - self i - n them._____ The

Bu - ddha, the Pa - tri-archs, they a - re i - n me, and when I

look, I see my - self i - n them._____ I a - m a

con - ti - nu - a - tio - n of my mo - the -

r and my fa - the - r. I a - m a

con - ti - nu - a - tio - n of all my blood an - ce-stors.

vio- le - nce in me.   I am de-ter-mined not to wa-ter the seeds of

cra- ving, a - ver-sion, and vio-le - nce in o - the - rs.   With re - solve and

with   com - pa - ssio - n,   I give ri - se to

this a-spi-ra - tio - n: May my prac-tice be an o-ff'ring of the heart.

May my prac-tice be an o - ff'ring of the heart.

Glossary

Akshayomati—Bodhisattva of Infinite Thought.

Asravas—All phenomena can be categorized as asrava, "with leaks," or anasrava, "without leaks." When our actions are "asrava," they don't yet have the nature of true insight and liberation, so they create more seeds of delusion in our mind. When our actions are "anasrava," they produce no unwholesome karmic fruit.

asura—A god or spirit who is fond of fighting and subject to frequent outbursts of anger.

Avalokiteshvara or Avalokita—Bodhisattva of Compassion and Deep Listening. Avalokita in the hungry ghost realm is a fierce manifestation of Avalokita with a face that is on fire.

bell of mindfulness—The sound of a bell or a clock, an electric beeper, or even the ring of a telephone that is used to call an individual or the community back to their breathing and the practice of mindfulness.

bhikkhu (Pali), bhikshu (Sanskrit)—One who seeks alms, referring to monks who have received full ordination (as opposed to novice ordination).

bhikkhuni (Pali), bhikshuni (Sanskrit)—One who seeks alms, referring to nuns who have received full ordination (as opposed to novice ordination).

bodhicitta—The awakening mind. Sometimes translated as the Mind of Love, because it is our awakened nature that impels us to love beings unconditionally and our understanding that enables us to do this.

Bodhisattva—("Bodhisattvebhyah" is the dative plural meaning "to the bodhisattvas.") Literally "enlightened being," one committed to enlightening oneself and others so that all may be liberated from suffering.

brahmacarya—A holy life in harmony with the mindfulness trainings; chastity, especially the celibate life of a Buddhist monk or nun.

Buddha—("Buddhaya" is the dative singular meaning "to the Buddha.") The Awakened One. Refers also to the capacity within every being to be "awake" or "enlightened."

cakravartin—World ruler, universal monarch.

chiliocosm—Inconceivably vast space. Thousand-world universe, each world having a Mount Sumeru, sun, moon, and four continents surrounded by oceans.

deva—Celestial being, angel.

Dharma—("Dharmaya" is the dative singular meaning "to the Dharma.") The true teachings of the Awakened One, the path of understanding and love.

dharma—Phenomenon, thing, object of mind.

Dharmadhatu—The entire cosmos of dharma elements. The underlying indestructible togetherness of the ultimate and historical dimensions.

Dharmakaya—The body of the Dharma; what remains when the historical Buddha is no longer with us. The true and ultimate reality.

discourse—A teaching given by the Buddha or one of his enlightened disciples ("sutra" in Sanskrit, "sutta" in Pali).

Eight Misfortunes—Obstacles to one's capacity to receive and practice the true teachings. To be (1) in the hell realms, (2) a hungry ghost, (3) an animal, (4) lazy when having excessive comforts, (5) ignorant without favorable conditions for awareness, (6) without hearing, sight, or speech,* (7) caught in arrogant speculation, (8) born before or after a Buddha's lifetime.

Eight Virtues—Eight virtues of water: clear, cool, sweet in taste, light in texture, sparkling bright, calm, eliminates hunger and thirst, and nourishes the practice.

Five Eyes—Physical eyes, deva eyes, Dharma eyes, wisdom eyes, Buddha eyes.

Five Faculties—Faith, energy, mindfulness, concentration, and wisdom.

Five Powers—Same as the Five Faculties, except that as powers they cannot be shaken by their opposites (e.g., energy cannot be swayed by laziness).

Five Skandhas—The five aspects of a person: form, feelings, perceptions, mental formations, and consciousness. Sometimes called Five Aggregates.

Fourfold Sangha—A practicing community of monks, nuns, laymen, and laywomen. See also Sangha.

Four Pairs and Eight Kinds of Holy People—Arhat, Non-Returner, Once-Returner, Stream-Enterer. The one who has attained the path heading toward the fruit and the one who has attained the fruit are considered one pair. Individually they are considered the Eight Types of Noble Ones.

Four Quarters—North, South, East, and West.

four ways of birth—From eggs, from a womb, by metamorphosis, and by division.

Four Wisdoms—Great Mirror Wisdom, Wisdom of Equality, Wisdom of Deep Looking, and Wisdom of Perfect Realization.

Gate gate paragate parasamgate bodhi svaha—The mantra from the Heart of the Prajnaparamita, uttered by Avalokiteshvara, meaning: "Gone, gone, gone all the way over, gone with all beings to the other shore, enlightenment, rejoice!"

gatha—A short poem or verse that we can recite during our daily activities to help us dwell in mindfulness.

hungry ghost—Preta, a being without faith or belief who ceaselessly craves without satisfaction.

Indra's Net—A limitless net stretching infinitely in all directions, with a jewel in each eye of the net. These jewels are infinite in number, each reflecting in itself all other jewels. This image is taken from the Avatamsaka Sutra and is generally used to illustrate the teachings of interbeing and interpenetration.

*Considered a limitation at the time of the Buddha.

kalpa—An inconceivably long time, an eon.

Kshitigarbha—Earth Store Bodhisattva, who vows to save beings in the realms of greatest suffering.

Lotus Throne—Seat of a Buddha.

mahasattva—Great Being, one who has realized the highest truths.

mandarava—Flowers that fall from the sky in the Pure Land, Sukhavati.

Manjushri —Bodhisattva of Understanding.

Manasarovara Lake—Also known as Anavatapta Lake, meaning cool, where there exists no heat of the afflictions.

Mara—The tempter, the Evil One, the killer, the opposite of the Buddha nature in each person; sometimes personalized as a deity. The obstacles to our practice, which arise in our own minds.

mindfulness trainings (formerly "precepts")—Guidelines offered by the Buddha to protect us and help us live in mindfulness, in the form of precepts prescribing a particular course of conduct.

mudra of peace—Also known as Seal of Peace, the sign made with the right hand when blessing water. The thumb joins the tip of the bent fourth finger while the second, third, and fifth fingers are held straight.

Naga King—A water deity governing springs, rain, rivers, lakes, and oceans.

Nagapushpa Assembly—The assembly that gathers around the Dragon Flower Tree to hear the teachings of Maitreya, the Buddha-to-be.

Namo—A phrase uttered when paying homage or respect to someone or something.

Namo Tassa Bhagavato Arahato Samma Sambuddhassa—"Homage to him, the World-Honored One, who is worthy of offerings, the One endowed with Perfect Understanding."

nirvana—The extinction of all views and concepts and the suffering based on them, to have no attachments to the realm of birth and death. Refers to the ultimate reality.

Prajnaparamita—Perfection of Wisdom, crossing to the other shore with understanding.

Pure Land— Sukhavati, the land of great happiness where the Buddha Amitabha dwells. An ideal place to practice the path of liberation.

Roseapple Island—Jambudvipa; an ancient name for India, the continent where humans live. From jambu, meaning roseapple tree.

Sadaparibhuta—The Bodhisattva Never Despising, or Never Disparaging.

Samantabhadra—Bodhisattva of Great Action, who made the ten great vows of practice.

samsara—Cycle of birth and death.

Sangha—("Sanghaya" is the dative singular meaning "to the sangha.") The Community that endeavors to practice the true teachings in harmony.

Sanghakaya—The collective body of the sangha.

Shakyamuni—(" Shakyamunaye" is the dative singular meaning "to Shakyamuni.") Literally, "sage of the Shakya clan." Refers to the historical Buddha whose awakening and teachings laid the foundation for the practice of Buddhism.

Six Dark Paths—Gods, humans, asuras, hells, hungry ghosts, animals.

Six Miracles (The Six Miraculous Powers)—(1) To see a great distance, (2) to hear all sounds, (3) to know one's past lives, (4) to perceive others' thoughts, (5) to travel anywhere at will, (6) to take on any form at will.

Six Tastes—Sweet, sour, salty, pungent, bitter, and astringent.

Sugata—Well-Gone One, one who has lived and practiced skillfully; another name for the Buddha.

Tathagata—One who comes from nowhere and goes nowhere, an epithet the Buddha used when referring to himself.

Ten Directions—Eight compass directions plus above and below. Refers to the entire universe.

Ten Stages—Bhumi, the stages through which a bodhisattva passes on the path of awakening.

Ten Unwholesome Deeds—Killing, stealing, sexual misconduct, lying, deceiving, exaggerating, contradicting, coveting, being angry, having wrong views.

Three Actions—Actions of body, speech, and mind.

Three Baskets—Tripitaka: discourses (sutras), precepts (vinaya), and commentaries on the Buddha's teachings (abhidharma).

Three Bodies of Buddha—Dharmakaya (body of true nature), Sambhogakaaya (body of bliss or enjoyment), Nirmanakaya (transformation body).

Three Jewels, Three Gems, Triple Gem—Buddha, Dharma, Sangha.

Three Paths of Suffering—Hells, hungry ghosts, animals.

Three Qualities (of food)—Sattva (purity), rajas (fiery energy), and tamas (dullness).

Three Realms—Form, formlessness, desire.

Three Times—Past, present, future.

Three Virtuous Positions of the Bodhisattva Path—Dwelling firmly in the practice (ten abodes), manifesting right actions (ten actions), and transferring all merit to the liberation of all beings (ten offerings).

Two Truths—The absolute truth and the relative truth. The absolute truth cannot be expressed directly in words and concepts, while the relative truth can. According to the absolute truth,s there is no self. However, the absolute and relative truths inter-are; there cannot be one without the other.

upasaka m., upasika f.—Layman or laywoman practitioner. Literally, "one who is close," i.e., practices closely with monks and nuns.

Vulture Peak—Grdhrakuta. The mountain near the town of Rajagriha where the Buddha sometimes stayed and taught.

yaksha—A ghost or demon, usually harmful but sometimes a protector of the Dharma.

Monastics and visitors practice the art of mindful living in the tradition
of Thich Nhat Hanh at our mindfulness practice centers around the world.
To reach any of these communities, or for information about how individuals,
couples, and families can join in a retreat, please contact:

Plum Village
33580 Dieulivol, France
plumvillage.org

Magnolia Grove Monastery
Batesville, MS 38606, USA
magnoliagrovemonastery.org

Blue Cliff Monastery
Pine Bush, NY 12566, USA
bluecliffmonastery.org

Deer Park Monastery
Escondido, CA 92026, USA
deerparkmonastery.org

**European Institute of Applied
Buddhism**
D-51545 Waldbröl, Germany
eiab.eu

Thailand Plum Village
Nakhon Ratchasima
30130 Thailand
thaiplumvillage.org

Asian Institute of Applied Buddhism
Ngong Ping
Lantau Island, Hong Kong
pvfhk.org

Maison de l'Inspir
77510 Villeneuve-sur-Bellot
France
maisondelinspir.org

Healing Spring Monastery
77510 Verdelot, France
healingspringmonastery.org

Nhap Luu–Stream Entering Monastery
Porcupine Ridge
Victoria 3461, Australia.
nhapluu.org

Mountain Spring Monastery
Bilpin, NSW 2758, Australia
mountainspringmonastery.org

**PARALLAX
PRESS**

Parallax Press, a nonprofit publisher founded by
Zen Master Thich Nhat Hanh, publishes books and media
on the art of mindful living and Engaged Buddhism.
We are committed to offering teachings that help transform
suffering and injustice. Our aspiration is to contribute
to collective insight and awakening, bringing about a
more joyful, healthy, and compassionate society.

Parallax Press
2236B Sixth Street
Berkeley, CA 94707
parallax.org

The Mindfulness Bell, a journal of the art of mindful living in the tradition
of Thich Nhat Hanh, is published two times a year by our community.
To subscribe or to see the worldwide directory of Sanghas
(local mindfulness groups), visit **mindfulnessbell.org**.